A MATTER OF Trust

THE IMPORTANCE OF PERSONAL INSTRUCTIONS

PEGGY R. HOYT J.D., M.B.A. AND CANDACE M. POLLOCK, J.D.

FOREWARD BY JACQUELINE J. POWERS

I

A Matter of Trust: The Importance of Personal Instructions
Copyright © 2005 Peggy R. Hoyt and Candace M. Pollock
ISBN 0-9719177-4-4

Published by Legacy Planning Partners, LLC
254 Plaza Drive
Oviedo, Florida 32765
Phone (407) 977-8080
Facsimile (407) 977-8078

Dedication

This book is dedicated to our clients

and their professional advisors who understand

that the legacy we leave is as much

about our carefully crafted personal instructions

as it is about the dollar amount received.

For more information or to order a copy of this book,
visit www.AMatterOfTrust.info
or call 407.977.8080 or 216.861.6160

Cover Photo is Maggie Kinnick and daughter, Pat Eguia
Editing by Debbie Roser, J.D.

Book Design by Julie Hoyt Dorman
www.dormangraphics.com

Table of Contents

A MATTER OF *Trust*

FOREWARD

The motivation for this book came from a true story about my friend, Margaret "Maggie" J. Kinnick, her daughter, Patricia "Pat" Eguia and Maggie's Revocable Living Trust. Maggie did everything right—or so she thought. She prepared an estate plan, a revocable living trust that was intended to provide for her during her lifetime and for her loved ones in the event of her death. However, something went wrong—terribly wrong.

Maggie always believed that her daughter, Pat, would outlive her. That's what every parent wishes for in their hearts. This was not, however, to be. Pat died first. After Pat died, Maggie had no relatives and only a few friends.

For years Maggie had conducted her banking activities with a local bank. As a result of this long-term relationship, when Pat died Maggie felt comfortable that everything would be fine if the bank was named as the successor trustee for her living trust. They would take good care of her when she could no longer take care of herself. In my opinion, the reality could not have been further from the truth.

Maggie's story is based upon the neglect, abandonment and lack of care provided by her successor trustee, a corporate trustee. Maggie was abandoned in life, and in death, by the company she trusted the most. To this company she had delegated all of her decisions—decisions related to her health, her quality of life, her real and personal property, her financial affairs and ultimately, her death.

Her corporate trustee, in its role as successor trustee to Maggie in her revocable living trust, effectively became her financial advisor, accountant, tax expert, real estate expert, appraisal expert, personal property expert, guardian, healthcare proxy, funeral director and personal representative. And, sadly Maggie paid them for this privilege. This is Maggie's story—hopefully, after reading it, it won't be yours.

Acknowledgements

I would like to thank Sister Francis Inez Redman, retired principal of Little Flower School, Great Mills, Maryland, for her many reviews and corrections to my original manuscript.

I would like to thank Lou Ellen Bell for typing and editing my original notes. I would also like to thank all of my friends who politely and patiently listened to me tell "Maggie's Story" over and over again. I appreciate everyone who encouraged me to "put this in writing so that others can prepare more properly." Finally, I would like to thank Peggy Hoyt and Candice Pollock who were able to turn my desire to make this information available into a reality.

—*Jacqueline J. Powers*

A MATTER OF *T*rust

Introduction

On one level, this book tells the story about a woman—Maggie Kinnick—of comfortable financial means, who placed her trust in the advice and guidance of others and paid them to look after her and her finances when she could no longer take care of herself and no family members were available to do so. She had taken pains to arrange her affairs and leave instructions about how her finances were to be used for her own needs. She authorized professionals to act on her behalf and for her benefit. Ironically, Maggie's legal and financial directives were probably more extensive than the directives most people in the United States have, yet they still failed to protect her in important ways.

Maggie was not well-served by her agents and as it turns out, her trust instructions were badly interpreted, but not for all of the predictable reasons you might expect. This is not a story about scheming advisors who embezzled her money or who invested in risky ventures and lost her money. This is a story about a woman who relied on pretty typical and straightforward legal directives to empower her agents to act on her behalf. Her legal advisors incorporated well-tested words and phrases in her healthcare and financial proxies. These seemingly straightforward legal directives and standard words and phrases have withstood the test of time and gave her agents discretion to perform a number of acts on her behalf. But, despite the standard "treatment," her directives did not give something essential—the guidance her advisors would need to know, specifically when discretion should be exercised and when her agents should refrain from acting.

In other words, Maggie's directives were *generic* and her agents dealt with her in a generic manner—conservatively and technically correct in the legal sense but not in ways she probably would have wanted in light of her circumstances. Her agents provided for her physical needs in basic ways that kept her safe but she was denied a quality of life that might otherwise have been available to her, with her own money, had she provided greater guidance to her agents.

Maggie's story serves as an illustration of how and where you need to give careful attention regarding your legal and financial directives to properly guide those you empower to act on your behalf. This book is intended to explore the pros and cons of the estate planning process and the standard directives used in estate planning, especially trust-based plans, so you can better understand how the instructions you give to your agents may fail to achieve your goals. We will share stories with you, both good and bad, of estate plans that accomplished the purpose for which they were created and some that did not.

We will discuss the need for planning for mental incapacity and the issues related to planning for death—a fate we all share. In both cases, we will explore the legal tools or directives that might best accomplish your planning goals. We will share with you the importance of proper asset ownership and the significance of making sure those you cherish are educated about your estate plan and the importance of keeping your plan updated and maintained over time.

We hope to provide guidance and insights that will prepare you for the selection of the estate planning professionals suited to your needs. In addition, we will give you insights into selecting the most qualified agents and trustees—from individuals to corporate trustees—so you can have confidence in the quality of your selection.

In the end, we hope you will be a better educated and better informed consumer who can make better decisions regarding your estate planning options and the individuals or professionals you choose to place in a position of trust. It's important, because after all, it is *a matter of trust.*

Chapter 1

Maggie's Story

This is Maggie's story. Margaret "Maggie" J. Kinnick was the creator, sometimes referred to as the grantor, trustor, settlor or trustmaker of a revocable living trust agreement (also known simply as a living trust). She signed her living trust on November 20, 1985, a little more than a year after Maggie's only child, Pat, died. When Maggie died on June 3, 1995, ten years after she created her trust, her bank had been serving as her successor trustee for seven years (since 1988). Maggie died alone, without her family, and spent the last years of her life without the care and services she deserved and could afford.

The purpose of Maggie's story is to demonstrate that a living trust, as well as other legal directives, although prepared by professionals and perhaps legally and technically correct in all respects, may not actually reflect the true wishes and desires of its creator. In Maggie's case, her trust appeared to be written for the sole benefit of the drafter, a corporate bank trustee. In reality, it should have been written for the benefit of its creator and sole beneficiary, Maggie. This book is designed to provide a foundation on which everyday people, people like you, can make educated and informed decisions about living trusts and their estate planning choices.

Maggie did what so many others like her do—she created a revocable living trust at a time in her life when her health was good and the future seemed stable. She may have attended a seminar, a workshop or met a legal or financial professional that described for her the benefits of a living trust. Many professionals promote living trust planning by describing the trust's ability to avoid probate or reduce estate taxes at the time of death. Some professionals may even explain the benefits of a revocable living trust in terms of disability planning or the ability to avoid a guardianship proceeding, also called a "living probate." These characteristics of a trust are all benefits to be derived from the living trust planning process. The challenge becomes making sure that the trust you create today continues to reflect your hopes, dreams and desires for the future.

As long as Maggie was alive and well, Maggie acted as the trustee. During these years, Maggie experienced no problems with her trust. She paid her bills, made investment decisions and proceeded through life without really noticing that she had a living trust. She appreciated the fact that she would avoid probate—a court administered process that many believe costs too much, takes too long and is a totally public process. Maggie wanted to avoid these costs, delays and other administrative inconveniences.

Maggie may have also been secure in the knowledge that in the event she became mentally disabled the bank, as her successor trustee, would assume the responsibility for the day-to-day management of her affairs, including paying her bills and making her investment decisions. Maggie probably thought she could rest easy—she had done everything she had been advised to do regarding putting her final affairs in order. In addition, Maggie had friends and other people who cared for her and her well-being—surely no one would let anything happen to her.

Time can change everything. Within three years of creating her trust, Maggie's doctor, pursuant to the instructions in the trust agreement, certified Maggie was no longer capable of managing her financial affairs. The legal effect of this letter was to remove Maggie as current trustee of her trust and replace her with her bank and its trust department as successor trustee. The bank was now authorized to handle Maggie's financial affairs as well as her day-to-day care.

This is where the story gets interesting. Maggie's trust—the instructions she provided for her ongoing care in the event of her disability or death—consisted of *four* typewritten pages. These four pages were supposed to contain everything the bank trustees would ever need to know about providing for Maggie for the rest of her life. The unfortunate truth is that these four pages contained only the minimum generic legal language and provided little, if any, guidance to the bank trustees about Maggie's personal wishes as to how she wanted to be cared for.

When the bank trustee assumed its role as successor trustee, it also assumed the fiduciary responsibility for managing and preserving Maggie's assets consistent with the terms of her trust agreement. They were bound by the language of the document. Like many "boiler-plate" revocable living trusts, the standards of care set forth in the trust included words like "health, education and maintenance." Other common phrases are "provide for my general well-being."

Without further definition in the trust agreement, what do these words mean? What does health, education and maintenance include? Does "health" mean the trustee should provide the minimum amount of care that would preserve Maggie's health? Does it include doctor's visits, prescriptions, and hospital care? What about elective surgery, over-the-counter medicines and vacations to improve the status of Maggie's mental health? What else might the word "health" include?

What does "education" include? If Maggie wanted to go to college or attend an elder hostel program, would that be included in the definition of "education?"

Does "maintenance" mean anything that Maggie might need to maintain her standard of living? What is her current standard of living and what will be required to maintain it? Can she aspire to a higher standard of living? These and other questions become extremely important when someone other than the original trust creator assumes responsibility for the management of the trust assets.

When Maggie's bank trustee assumed responsibility for her trust, Maggie was still living at home. Home for Maggie was a comfortable lake front condominium in beautiful central Florida. However, it wasn't long before the bank trustee determined that the cost of maintaining Maggie in her home wasn't in Maggie's best interest and the condominium was sold and Maggie was moved to a nursing home. Did Maggie's instructions say she wanted to live in a nursing home? Or did they say that Maggie would prefer to remain in her own home, even if she was physically incapable of caring for herself? Did the trust say that the trustee should hire nursing staff or live-in care so that Maggie could remain in her home as long as possible? No. Maggie's trust said to provide for her health, education and maintenance.

Maggie's trust instructions failed because Maggie didn't know how the bank trustee would interpret "health, education and maintenance." She probably never even had a conversation with the attorney who created the trust about the consequences of using a health, education and maintenance standard in the event of disability. Undoubtedly, Maggie never considered the possibility of leaving hand-written or type-written instructions that she could create to give greater guidance to her trustee regarding how she really wanted to be cared for in the event of disability. Maggie may never even have contemplated the idea that she might become disabled during her lifetime. Our experience indicates that most of our clients believe that disability is not a reality for them— it always happens to someone else. Most of our clients assume they will die in their sleep—peacefully, with no problems and no period of disability. The reality is far from this utopian view.

Another issue Maggie failed to consider is the longevity of her bank trustee. When Maggie created her trust agreement she was doing business with her local bank. After it assumed responsibility as Maggie's successor trustee, the local bank was acquired by a larger bank. The local trust officer was no longer assigned to Maggie's trust account. Not once, but many times over the years Maggie's trust officer was replaced. It wasn't long before the trust officer assigned to Maggie's account had never met Maggie, didn't know Maggie from Adam's dog and certainly had no appreciation for Maggie's hopes, dreams, aspirations and goals. There were no notes or conversations memorializing the ways that Maggie might want to be cared for in the event of her disability and the language of the trust offered no guidance. Maggie's trust officer didn't know (or care) whether Maggie had new clothes to wear, enjoyed a cocktail at the dinner hour or received piano lessons to help her pass the time. There was no written schedule to indicate how often Maggie wanted to have her hair done or how it was to be done, whether she enjoyed a manicure and a massage or any of the other small details that might have made Maggie's life more comfortable and enjoyable.

The bank trustee's primary responsibility was fiduciary in nature requiring the bank to preserve the assets of the trust—a goal that may have ultimately been incompatible with what Maggie might really want—to enjoy her money for her sole benefit, even if it meant that the principal wasn't preserved and there wasn't a dime left at the time of her death. Who was she saving her money for anyway? Her only child had predeceased her and she had no other close relatives that she wished to benefit. Even if she did, she probably wouldn't have benefited other family members at the expense of her own lifetime comfort.

It's hard to blame the bank trustees for upholding their fiduciary responsibility—the responsibility to preserve and manage Maggie's assets. When a corporate or bank trustee has limited guidance—only "health, education and maintenance" to go on—how can we say they didn't do what they were required to do? Maggie lived in a nursing home facility that provided for her basic needs. She had clothing, albeit old and worn; she had a wheelchair, even though it was the least expensive model available; she was fed three times a day, even if it was institutional food; and she was bathed and had her hair cut on a regular basis, even if it wasn't consistent with what Maggie might have done for herself.

The only person that was concerned about the care Maggie was receiving was her daughter's friend, Jacqueline Powers. Jacqueline saw more than the words "health, education and maintenance" on the page. She saw the real Maggie. She knew the Maggie that loved music, the theater, flower gardens, walks in the park, a waterfront view, excellent food and a glass of wine with dinner, beautiful clothes, and perfectly coifed hair and manicured nails. Jacqueline didn't see Maggie as a failing older woman banished to a nursing home for the purpose of living out her final days with only the bare essentials to support her daily lifestyle.

Without Jacqueline, Maggie would not have enjoyed a number of the luxuries that Jacqueline secured for her. Jacqueline saw to it that Maggie had candy in a dish by her bed, that she had a wine cooler at dinner, that she received piano lessons, participated in outings, had new clothes, a tree at Christmas and a few presents and cards for special occasions. Many of these items Jacqueline purchased with her own money—as gifts to a friend—because despite Jacqueline's efforts she couldn't convince the bank trustee that these niceties could improve the quality of Maggie's life and were still consistent with her written trust instructions. Rest assured, it wasn't because Maggie couldn't afford these little extras. At the time of Maggie's death, her trust account had a value of nearly half a million dollars!

Maggie died alone. Her daughter died years before. She had no family by her side. The only person who cared was Jacqueline.

Jacqueline was notified by the funeral home that Maggie had died and that her body had been transferred from the nursing home to a funeral home. Jacqueline had been listed as her next-of-kin even though she was not legally related to Maggie. The funeral home wanted to know what to do with Maggie regarding her funeral arrangements. Maggie had not made any advance arrangements—she had not planned her service, written her obituary, left any parting words and there were no instructions regarding her final wishes for a memorial service. Maggie had, however, pre-purchased a cremation certificate, urn and memorial niche. This was done when her daughter Pat died so that mother and daughter could be together for eternity. Had Pat not died first, almost certainly, Maggie would not have planned and paid for her cremation.

As a result, Jacqueline planned and paid for Maggie's memorial service. The bank trustee refused to pay for the memorial service despite the fact that the trust instructions gave the trustee discretion to pay for, "my funeral, burial and last illness expenses." In this case, the bank exercised its discretion *not* to pay for these expenses. The only people in attendance were Jacqueline, a representative from the funeral home, and the man who opened the memorial niche.

Although the bank trustee was advised of the service, no bank representative was in attendance. There were no flowers at the service because Maggie's trust instructions failed to specifically provide for their cost and, again, the bank trustee exercised its discretion not to expend trust assets for this purpose.

When the memorial niche was opened, Jacqueline discovered that Pat's ashes were not in the niche. It was later discovered that Pat's ashes were in storage at the bank. Maggie's instructions that Pat's ashes be maintained and preserved until such time as she passed away had been overlooked or misplaced. When Jacqueline made the discovery that Pat's ashes were missing, she requested that the bank trustee deliver Pat's ashes and authorize the re-opening of the niche so that mother and daughter could rest in peace together.

The bank's response was unbelievable. Jacqueline was advised that the trust would not authorize the expenditure of any monies for the purpose of re-opening the niche and placing Pat's ashes inside. The bank, however, did not object to the continuing charge for maintaining Pat's ashes in their own vault.

In life as well as in death, Maggie's instructions failed to provide for her. She did the right thing—she created a set of legal directives that were intended to provide for her in the event of disability or death. These legal directives turned out to be wholly insufficient—not from a legal standpoint—but from a personal perspective. All the legal documents in the world are not going to protect us from ourselves. As consumers, we have to be informed about our choices—the options we have to provide comprehensive, personalized instructions that will do more than simply transfer our assets to a successor or beneficiaries in the event of our disability or death.

Maggie stands as the example—our poster child, if you will—of the average person of respectable means, who obtained legal and professional assistance and yet, still did not have what would have been considered protections that should have provided for a life well-lived—especially at the end, when it really counts. Join us on this journey through *A Matter of Trust* to learn what you and your loved ones can do to have a different experience.

A MATTER OF *Trust*

Chapter Two

A Matter of Trust

For many people, estate planning in general, and living trusts in particular, are shrouded in an aura of mystique. As a result, far too many avoid estate planning altogether. It's interesting, but as an optimistic people, it is common to hear someone say, "*When* I win the lottery," and "*If* I die." The reality is few of us experience a huge financial windfall, and none of us gets out of here alive. Why then are we so hesitant to plan for the one thing in life that's truly certain? Ben Franklin may have said it best back in 1789 when he announced, "Nothing is certain in life except death and taxes." This is still true today. The difference is change. Change in when and how we are dying and change in our structure of taxation. Will Rogers may have said it even better, "The difference between death and taxes is that death doesn't get worse every time Congress meets."

The problem may not be dying too soon, but living too long. The fact is we are living longer—often with uncertainty about what our quality of life will be. Stroke, dementia and Alzheimer's disease are all on the rise. Nursing homes have waiting lists and it seems there is an assisted living facility being constructed on every corner. The age group over 100 years is one of the fastest growing groups in our country. Peggy's grandfather celebrated his 102nd birthday on June 15, 2005 and is still doing well. Her great grandmother lived until she was 106 years old. If we don't construct estate plans for ourselves, what options exist? Can we rely on the protections of our state laws to provide a quality of life (or death) that will be consistent with our wants, needs, aspirations and desires? We don't think so.

There are many myths surrounding the need for estate planning and the protections that different legal tools and directives can provide. Most people believe that if they've done a will, they've done all they need to do to plan for their families. There is nothing further from the truth. No estate plan is complete without a full complement of legal directives that provide for unexpected mental disability—not as certain as death—but occurring with increasing frequency among people over 65 years. Having said that, currently the age group 16-64 years has more than five times the number of disabled individuals than the over 65 age group. Disability is not a disease of an older generation—it can affect all of us.

Everyone has an "estate plan" whether they know it or not and regardless of whether their assets are generous or modest. Few people realize they are doing estate planning every time they name a beneficiary on a retirement account or create a joint title on a deed to a house or bank account. Nevertheless, that is exactly what they are doing and the way they do it will have a dramatic effect on the ultimate disposition of their assets.

Estate planning basically boils down to creating a combination of legal directives to authorize others to manage and direct your affairs when and if you are mentally incapacitated, and at your death. Wills and trusts, healthcare proxies or surrogates and living wills, deeds and beneficiary forms are just some of the common directives that may be included in your estate plan. The number and type of directives can be complex or simple, depending on your needs, motivation, goals and budget.

The key to good estate planning is making sure your plan is complete and understanding how each directive supports or undermines your overall intentions. If your plan has gaps or conflicts, state laws will dictate what happens to you and your affairs. These laws may not be consistent with your wishes for your care and for the protection of your loved ones.

Proper estate planning can help you maintain control and independence as well as achieve your goals. To do this you need to 1) identify your goals for taking care of yourself and your loved ones when you are no longer available to do so—either through incapacity or death; 2) understand your planning options, including their costs; and 3) coordinate your directives to eliminate planning conflicts and gaps.

There are a number of goals legal directives can address. The most common are:

- Avoiding probate or guardianship
- Maintaining privacy
- Providing for minor children or grandchildren
- Providing for a spouse or life partner
- Providing for special needs family members in such a way that they remain eligible for public benefit programs
- Protecting assets from nursing home costs and other catastrophic illness costs
- Minimizing state and federal estate taxes

There is confusion about the effectiveness of wills as opposed to living trusts. Is one better than the other? If you have a living trust, do you also need a will? Who will you select as your personal representative or successor trustee? This book will answer all those questions and more.

Wills

A will is your written expression of your last wishes regarding what should happen to your property at your death. In other words, a will is a death-planning directive. A will is completely without power to direct your affairs in the event you become disabled during your lifetime. To plan for this possibility, other legal directives such as durable financial powers of attorney and durable healthcare powers of attorney are necessary.

Some people believe that creating a will helps you to avoid probate. Exactly the opposite is true. Creating a will and owning assets in your individual name guarantees probate—the court administered process of carrying out the terms and conditions of your will.

When people discuss estate planning, their first assumption is that they must do a will. This is only part of the story. A will may be a central component to a comprehensive estate plan but it is only one component. There are many others that we will discuss throughout the chapters of this book.

Living Trusts

Many people believe that a living trust offers "total protection" in the event of incapacity as well as death. Total protection may include protection from a forced guardianship in the event of mental incapacity, or the avoidance of probate at the time of death. Total protection may mean different things to different people. Total protection may, in reality, not offer any form of protection at all. The benefits to be derived from a living trust depend on a large number of factors including the creation or design of the trust, the drafting of the trust, the ownership of assets controlled by the trust and the actual instructions contained within or as an adjunct to the trust.

Many articles and books have been written about the advantages of having a living trust as the primary estate-planning tool instead of a will. In general, the books that support living trusts describe the benefits of a living trust in terms of the protections that may be provided in the event you become incapacitated during your lifetime. In addition, the literature advises when assets controlled by the trust are properly owned, a living trust can avoid probate—a dreaded result for many individuals. There can also be significant estate tax and asset protection advantages provided by proper trust planning.

Further, bank trust departments or corporate trust companies (also known as corporate trustees or corporate fiduciaries) are often recommended as excellent choices as trustees, either as initial trustee or as a successor trustee, in the event you become sick, disabled, or mentally incompetent; at the time of death; or if you just want someone else to handle your financial affairs. To provide support for enlisting the assistance of a bank or corporate trustee, many trust advocates promote the idea that banks and trust companies can theoretically never go out of business and the same people usually work there over a long period of time. This may have been true in the past but, today times are different. Financial institutions are merging at astronomical rates so the bank you deal with today may not be the bank you deal with tomorrow. Further, people are more mobile, switching from job to job and moving from state to state.

The popular reasons people create living trusts are:

1) **Privacy.** In theory no one will know what assets are owned by your trust. A trust is a private document that is not recorded in the public records and is not required to be reflected in the records of the probate court. Therefore, a trust can provide privacy for you and your beneficiaries.

2) **Avoid Delay.** Theoretically, there should be no delay in the distribution of your assets from a living trust to your beneficiaries after your death. One potential client told us that a living trust could be settled in less than an hour. The reality is that the trust administration process requires several steps—steps that are similar in nature to the probate process except they are done privately. These steps include gathering and valuing the trust assets, making sure all creditors and taxes have been fully paid and then distributing assets to the beneficiaries. This process can be short or long depending on the nature and complexity of the assets and the value of the estate.

3) **Currently Effective.** A living trust, unlike a will, is effective on the day it is created. You don't have to wait for disability or death for the value of the living trust to become apparent. A living trust allows you to manage your assets while you are alive and well, while setting up the instructions necessary to provide for you in the event of incapacity or death.

4) **Amendable and Revocable.** A revocable living trust is both amendable and revocable as long as you retain legal capacity. Nothing you include in your trust today can't be modified or changed in the future. This is especially important over time as the primary elements that will change in your life are the four

L's: *1)* Life, *2)* Law, *3)* Lawyer, and *4)* Legacy. Each of these elements is likely to change (and on a regular and recurring basis) in your life.

5) **Disability Protection.** If you become mentally incompetent, a trust can be designed to let the disability successor trustee "step into your shoes" and manage your financial affairs. This process helps avoid a court-administered guardianship proceeding whereby the court takes control of your financial affairs. We refer to guardianships as the worst possible kind of lawsuit—a lawsuit your family files against you to have you declared incompetent, you get to pay for the lawsuit and you lose all of your rights to manage your life and your financial affairs.

6) **Protection for Family Members.** A living trust can incorporate instructions for the creation of additional trusts that can protect your spouse or life partner, your children, disabled family members, and yes, even your pets. These additional trusts may provide tax relief or create creditor or asset protection. They can also provide protections in the event of divorce, catastrophic illness, bankruptcy or business failures. Trusts can protect heirs from themselves in the event of drug, alcohol or chemical dependency disorders and they can protect governmental benefits for disabled persons.

7) **Minimize Estate Taxes.** Drafted correctly, a married couple can maximize each individual's estate tax exemption and thereby minimize overall estate taxes. When the trust is properly drafted and the assets are correctly owned, the estate tax savings may amount to hundreds of thousands of dollars.

What attributes should you look for in a living trust? How do you tell a good trust from a bad trust? Is the trust you have well-written and designed to meet your needs? One way to begin answering these questions is to consider the process you experienced when you created your living trust. How did you first learn about living trusts? Did you do some self-study by reading books or articles on the topic? Did you attend a seminar? A workshop? Was the purpose of the workshop or seminar to provide you with information or sell you a product? Did your legal or financial professional suggest you consider living-trust based planning? After you made your first contact with the legal professional, how did the process proceed? Was there an educational base to the process or did you feel that your personal information was simply being entered into a word processor? Did you have an individual comprehensive design meeting that required your understanding and participation in the creation of your plan? Were the final documents fully explained to you before signing? Did you understand what you were signing and the legal effect of the document in the event of your disability or death? Were you asked to prepare any personally constructed documents to supplement your plan and provide for your well-being in the event of disability or death—documents like personal property memorandums, instructions to healthcare providers or successor trustees or memorial instructions?

Most people we meet who have previously prepared living trusts have no idea what their trust was designed to accomplish. Many have put their complete faith and trust in their bank or corporate trustee, their financial professional or their legal professional without a solid understanding of the legal effect of the documents they have created.

Some people cite the cost of creating and maintaining a trust as one of the primary disadvantages of trust planning. If you consider only the cost associated with having a trust drafted as its value, a trust might appear to be more costly than a will, for instance. However, if you look at the higher level of protection that trusts can give you and your loved ones during life, during disability and at death, trusts are very cost effective.

Trusts also require education regarding asset ownership. In order for your trust to control your assets and have your trust instructions apply, you must own your assets in the name of your trust or ensure that your trust is named as the beneficiary of your life insurance, annuities, retirement plans and other beneficiary designated assets.

Trusts can be created to accomplish a variety of goals. Therefore, you could have a revocable living trust and an irrevocable life insurance trust, and you could name different beneficiaries for the various trusts. This may seem a little overwhelming at first, but if you focus on the objectives you want to achieve, trusts usually offer some of the best solutions—if they are well-drafted and properly funded.

Personal Representatives and Successor Trustees

Regardless of whether you choose a will or a trust as your primary planning tool, you can't avoid the issue of personal representatives, also known as executors and/or successor trustees. A personal representative or executor is the individual(s) or company responsible for carrying out the responsibilities of administering your will when you die. A successor trustee is the individual(s) or company responsible for carrying out the duties of administering your trust when you become mentally incapacitated or die.

The selection of these individuals or companies can add to the success or failure of any estate plan. Many people select family members because of a perception that it will cost less to have an individual responsible for these duties. This may be true in some instances but can also be misguided if family members are not qualified, don't take their responsibilities seriously, mismanage estate or trust assets or discourage (rather than promote) family harmony.

The people named as personal representative or trustee are placed in the highest position of trust imaginable. They have to be able to "step into your shoes" and make decisions that are consistent with the decisions you would make if you were available to make them personally. They can only do this successfully if they first are qualified to handle the responsibility and second, are given comprehensive instructions that clearly outline their rights, responsibilities and duties.

The following chapters focus on each of the areas important to creating an estate plan that will protect you and those you cherish— one that works from a legal and technical perspective *and* from a personal basis.

Chapter 3

Planning for Your Disability

As we've said, our problem may not be dying too soon, but living too long. This statement points squarely at the issue of disability planning. In an estate planning environment, when we talk about disability planning we are generally referring to a mental disability rather than a physical disability. If you were to become physically disabled, the likelihood is that you could still manage your financial affairs and make your own medical care decisions. In the event of mental disability, however, you may not be able to make either financial decisions or personal healthcare decisions. In this event, it is imperative and even critical that you have proper legal directives in place to clearly state your preference regarding the selection of your agents or surrogates to make your decisions for you.

Recently in the news, the nation became aware of the ongoing battle between the parents of a young Florida woman, Terri Schiavo, and her husband-legal guardian. Terri had been in a coma since 1990 and was sustained through artificial means since that time. Terri's husband said she would never have wanted to be sustained this way. Her parents said she would have wanted to live and, in fact, had some brain activity that warranted sustaining her.

Both families, no doubt, spent countless hours of heartache and soul-searching in their attempt to do the right thing. They spent large sums for legal fees to have their perspective adopted by the courts. The medical experts offered opinions about her medical status. The courts struggled to determine what they were permitted to do under the law. We, as an on-looking public, might also have strong opinions about what should have been done.

Nowhere in this picture was a clear written statement from the young woman about whether or not she would like her life artificially prolonged under such conditions. And yet, part of the tragedy is that she had it within her power to express her wishes in the unlikely chance that just such a medical event might occur. Had she executed appropriate legal directives outlining her wishes, the battle between her parents and her husband could have been averted under most circumstances. At the very least, the courts would have had some indication of her intent.

Most people think estate planning only involves how their "stuff" is distributed when they die. Many, particularly younger people, don't get around to executing these disability directives because the chance of needing them seems slight. Good estate planning includes planning for potential periods of disability before death. As the tragedy of Terri Schiavo and her family show, disability can sometimes be worse than death for all involved.

The State's Default Plan

Most state statutes provide guidance in addressing mental disability issues. The guidance involves determining when a person is mentally incapacitated, who is authorized to act and the scope of the authorization. In general, the state laws will require the decision makers to look first to a named guardian appointed by the court; then to a spouse, if any; then to adult children; then to parents; then to adult relatives; and finally, somewhere further down the line, to close friends. For unmarried individuals, this close friend—sometimes called a life alliance partner—is the last on the list. This area is ripe for controversy, especially if your life alliance partner and your family don't enjoy a close relationship.

In the absence of written directives, the state laws will appoint someone to take care of you and your financial affairs if you become disabled and have no legal directives in place for this possibility. The person appointed is the "guardian" and the person the guardian is responsible for is called the "ward." There are other details to the state default plan that will be discussed more fully in the section under Guardianship in this chapter.

Avoiding the State's Default Plan

There are a number of legal directives you can prepare to name agents to handle your medical and financial affairs when you are unable to do so for yourself. Each state has laws regarding the formalities the directives must follow to be considered valid. Although some practitioners might use boilerplate, one-size-fits-all forms, there is actually a lot of variety you can request in your directives to fit your particular needs.

The legal directives fall into two categories: financial directives and healthcare directives. We discuss financial directives first because it has been our experience that this is one of the most overlooked areas of planning. Most people are familiar with healthcare directives, and many have them. However, we have found that it is not uncommon for clients to mistakenly think that their healthcare directives authorize their agents to handle their financial affairs. Nothing can be further from the truth.

Financial Directives

Powers of Attorney—Financial

A financial power of attorney is a directive that names the individual(s) you select to manage your financial affairs. Special rules apply to assets controlled by a living trust and are discussed later in the chapter. Agents named in such directives are fiduciaries with a legal duty to act for the benefit of the person who created the power of attorney. The fiduciary must use the highest degree of good faith when acting for the maker. This fiduciary duty doesn't permit the agent to place his own interests above the maker's interests and prevents the agent from self-dealing with the maker's assets. There are legal penalties when someone in a fiduciary position mismanages the assets of another person.

Despite these standards, financial powers must be carefully drafted to avoid giving too little or too much authority to agents. What may be too much authority for one family might not be enough authority in another family. Therefore, you should have a detailed conversation with your legal advisor regarding what you want and need to accomplish if you are unable to handle your own financial affairs due to mental incapacity. Here are some factors you need to consider when deciding what provisions should be in your directives.

Durable vs. Not Durable. It seems counter-intuitive, but unless a financial power states that it is "durable," it loses its power when the maker becomes mentally incapacitated. Therefore, only a Durable Financial Power of Attorney is useful when planning for mental incapacity.

Some financial institutions can raise objections to honoring the agent's acts under a power of attorney on the grounds that the power is stale, meaning that it was executed too long ago for the institution to feel comfortable with its validity. State laws can have specific rules determining whether financial institutions have a legitimate legal basis to challenge older powers of attorney. The irony here is that if the power of attorney is determined to be too old and the maker must execute a new one, and the maker is now incapacitated, the purpose for which the durable power of attorney was created in the first place has been thwarted. In this event, a court-ordered guardianship may be the only solution.

Immediate vs. Springing. A durable power of attorney that is effective immediately has pros and cons. On the pro side, your named agent can use the power of attorney to act on your behalf as soon as the document is signed. Therefore, if you sign the power of attorney and your named agent needs to act on your behalf immediately, he or she is authorized to do so.

This can be good news or bad news. We've already said that the good news is that it works now. The bad news is that your agent may use the power of attorney in a way that you are not happy with. An immediately effective durable power of attorney has the same effect as taking out your checkbook, signing a number of blank checks and handing the checkbook over to your agent. This works great if you have a good, trusting relationship with your agent. It may be a concern, however, for those who have to think long and hard in order to name someone they can trust in this capacity.

You might decide that it is better to have a springing power of attorney—one that doesn't become effective until you're no longer capable of making your own financial decisions. Again, there is good news and bad news associated with a springing power of attorney. The good news is that you have increased protections against agents using the power when you are still capable of making your own decisions. The bad news is that now they have to jump through a few hurdles in order to show that the disability triggering event has occurred. The agent will need to satisfy financial institutions or individuals to whom the power of attorney is presented that you are disabled. How do they do this? Well, they'll probably have to obtain and then present some written documentation of disability. Generally this documentation will be provided in the form of a letter or letters from your doctor(s) indicating you are no longer capable of managing your own financial affairs. Your agent will be responsible for obtaining this documentation and presenting it along with the power of attorney to demonstrate their ability to serve as your agent.

This is an example of what might happen. Your named agent goes to your bank and presents the springing power of attorney with a written letter from two doctors documenting the mental incapacity of the principal (you—the person who gave the power of attorney). The bank teller, manager or customer relations manager generally doesn't have the authority to decide whether this evidence is sufficient. They might then direct the agent to the bank's legal department, usually not located on site and many times not even located in the same state. The legal department will then need an attorney who is familiar with your state law so they can make a determination of the validity of the document. And this will take, what do you think—minutes, hours or days? We're betting on the latter. As a result, the springing power of attorney might not be the best solution for you. They provide a measure of protection, however, that must be weighed against the complexity of use.

As an alternative, you might consider an immediately effective power of attorney but ask your attorney if he or she will hold the power of attorney in escrow until your agent can provide proof to your attorney that you are disabled. Again, this may take longer than you want. It's always a balancing act—complexity versus protection. You need to decide what works best for your situation.

Limited vs. General. The role of the durable financial power of attorney is to manage financial assets. Powers of attorney can be limited or they can be general in nature. Limited powers of attorney list the specific category of acts the agent can perform for the maker, like sell real estate and make tax elections.

General powers of attorney allow the agent to handle essentially all financial transactions on behalf of the principal. General durable financial powers of attorney are generally preferred because you may not always be able to predict the circumstances under which the power of attorney will be required. Boilerplate powers of attorney are generally inadequate when it comes to describing those events for which the power of attorney will be required.

Typical acts that can be authorized under a general power of attorney are the ability to sell or lease a home; prepare your income taxes; represent you in a lawsuit for the purpose of bringing the suit or settling an existing suit; and make gifts on your behalf for planning purposes, just to name a few. Your average off-the-shelf power of attorney does not address all of these situations and rarely addresses the situations for which you will actually need the power of attorney in the first place. It is recommended that you "plan for the worst and hope for the best, because anything else is just wishful thinking." In the legal world, what can go wrong will. Therefore, your best defense is to have estate planning directives that contemplate the unusual and worst-case scenario.

Unlimited vs. Limited Gifting (amount & recipients). The self-dealing rules governing agents prohibit them from giving the maker's assets to themselves or family without specific authority in the directive to do so. The power of attorney should clearly state the scope of the gifting authority including the identity of recipients, specific gift amount, gift formula or unlimited gifting authority. Gifting authority can be a strategy to reduce estate taxes or for long-term care asset protection in the event you require nursing home care.

Dual Agents vs. Alternate Agents. The maker can have one, two or more agents authorized to act, or have someone identified as "runner-up" when the initial agent can't serve. Problems can arise when two authorized agents disagree or if third parties require proof of the first agent's inability to serve. Appropriate language in the power of attorney can indicate that even when there are two agents named, only one is required to make decisions. This may be useful if you have children you want to name as co-agents but the complexity of requiring two signatures for each transaction may be too cumbersome. In addition, if dual agents are unable to agree on decisions in the best interest of the maker, then unnecessary litigation and other problems may arise. It is rarely a good idea to name only one agent without naming a "runner up" who can serve as your agent when the first person can't serve as your agent.

Revoking a Power of Attorney. You can revoke a power of attorney at any time while you are mentally competent. However, communicating to others that you have revoked your power of attorney can become difficult. To revoke a power of attorney, you need to execute a written revocation and then deliver a copy of the revocation to any financial institution or third party that might have been given the power initially.

You may also have to file a copy of your power of attorney with a county recorder's office if you want financial institutions to rely on your agent's authority regarding the sale of real estate. In this way, the financial institution or third party can inspect the public record to verify that the agent under the power has the authority to perform the sale of the property. If you have filed a power of attorney with the recorder's office and you later want to revoke the power, you will need to file a copy of the revocation with the recorder's office as well, so third parties are on notice that the power has been revoked.

These considerations should underscore that there is a lot of decision making that goes into drafting a financial power of attorney that meets the specific needs and concerns of an individual. Selection of the agents and the scope of their powers are crucial to achieving your goals and managing your affairs when you are no longer able to do so. Everyone should have a financial power of attorney.

Healthcare Directives

Healthcare directives authorize agents to make medical decisions for you when you are mentally incapacitated. The directives can have different names in different jurisdictions. The generic names are "healthcare power of attorney," "healthcare proxy" or "healthcare surrogate." The directives come into play in two separate circumstances: *1)* Every day medical care decisions, and *2)* End of life determinations.

Living Will for Heroic or Life-Sustaining Medical Treatment

The directive referred to as a "living will" in many jurisdictions is created to provide written instructions stating whether the maker wants life-sustaining treatment or procedures withheld or withdrawn if they are unable to make informed medical decisions and are in a *terminal condition* or in a *permanently unconscious state*. Comfort care, such as medication, can be continued if it is to reduce pain, even if the maker chose not to authorize life-sustaining treatment.

The living will also permits you to specify whether or not you want artificially or technologically supplied food and water. These will be provided unless you specifically indicate you do not want them.

The living will names the people you want to act as your agents regarding life-sustaining decisions. The agents cannot override your instructions in the living will but it makes sense to discuss your wishes with potential agents to make sure the named agents can make difficult decisions, if necessary. You should select someone you trust, who understands your wishes regarding the termination of life and will have the emotional fortitude to carry through. We love the story of a friend who said he could never choose his wife for this role because she loved him too much. Instead, he selected his sister, who he says, "never liked him very much anyway."

A well-drafted living will specifically defines the terms it uses in order to reduce potential dispute over your intended definitions. One example is the use of the word "persistent vegetative state." If you want to continue all forms of life-sustaining treatment, including cardio-pulmonary resuscitation (CPR), you should clearly state your medical preferences in writing. If your agent is authorized to execute a DNR or "do not resuscitate" order, you should say so. If you have particular religious or other concerns about the use of blood transfusions or other matters, you should also clearly state your instructions and preferences in this directive.

Durable Healthcare Power of Attorney (Healthcare Surrogate)

Situations can occur when you might be unable to speak for yourself but you don't meet the criteria for invoking a living will with its life-terminating implications. For instance, you might experience a stroke that temporarily makes you unable to speak or makes you mentally incapacitated. In this event, you will need someone to sign medical consent forms and authorize your medical providers regarding your medical care. The directive for this situation is often called a durable healthcare power of attorney or healthcare surrogate.

The purpose of this directive is to identify the agents who are authorized to make most healthcare decisions for you if you lose the capacity to make informed healthcare decisions for yourself. The proxies are generally not effective until you are unable to make your own healthcare decisions. The types of decisions that can be made with a durable healthcare power of attorney are everyday type medical care decisions, like consent to surgery, consent to treatment, transfer to or from a medical facility, the hiring and firing of nurses, doctors and therapists, and the release of medical information and records.

You can authorize or limit the specific types of healthcare decisions your agent can make for you. For instance, you could authorize the agent to consent to surgical procedures for you but limit the agent's ability to move you to a different healthcare facility. You can include specific directions for your agents regarding healthcare decisions that invoke religious beliefs, such as blood transfusions or other procedures.

Health Information Portability and Accountability Act (HIPAA)

A durable healthcare power of attorney has become especially important in light of the recently implemented regulations under the Health Information Portability and Accountability Act (HIPAA) that became effective in June 2003. Under HIPAA, you must name a "personal representative" for the purpose of transacting business on your behalf with your healthcare providers and insurers.

For those of you already familiar with HIPAA, it may have caused you problems. For us, Peggy was unable to obtain a copy of her own contact lens prescription when out of town on business because she had failed to designate such an individual in advance, in writing, at her doctor's office. It didn't matter that she was giving them verbal authorization over the phone. A client with a husband in the hospital in a coma called when she needed to contact the husband's insurance company to discuss his benefits eligibility. The insurance company refused to talk with her because she was not the insured. He was clearly unable to communicate on his own behalf, yet she had not been properly designated as his personal representative as required by HIPAA. Protect yourself and make sure your healthcare power of attorney contains proper instructions to nominate your healthcare surrogate as your personal representative under the provisions of HIPAA.

There is a debate in some legal circles as to whether a separate directive is required to meet the standards required by HIPAA. You should discuss this with your legal advisor to determine whether it makes sense to prepare a separate directive to satisfy potential challenges as to whether your healthcare proxies comply with HIPAA— just to be on the safe side. The separate directive normally will be a statement authorizing the agents named in the healthcare proxies to make decisions consistent with the authority under HIPAA.

Visitation in Healthcare Facilities

Some healthcare facilities restrict visitors to immediate family when a patient is in intensive care or other instances where medical circumstances dictate limiting visits. Family is defined by most facilities as next of kin. This could cause unnecessary distress if close friends or companions are not permitted to visit under these restrictions.

You should include a specific authorization regarding the people who will be permitted to visit you when visitation is normally restricted to next of kin. You should consult with your legal advisor to decide whether this type of authorization should be incorporated in the durable healthcare power of attorney or whether it should be a separate document. If the directive is a separate document, you should make sure it complies with the same legal formalities as the durable healthcare power of attorney. This directive should also specify that it is "durable" to ensure that it retains its legal authority during any period in which you have lost mental capacity.

Legal Formalities

State laws on healthcare proxies require they be executed with certain legal formalities. The formalities can differ from state to state. Generally, they should be signed before a notary and/or before two disinterested witnesses who are present when you sign your name. The following people are generally ineligible to be witnesses to these proxies: anyone who is related to you by blood, marriage or adoption; your attorney-in-fact (someone with a financial power of attorney); and your doctor or the administrator of any nursing home in which you are receiving care. Usually, copies of the properly executed forms are as good as an original.

If you are a "snow bird" who regularly travels to another state, it is advisable that you make sure your directives comply with the standards of that state as well as your home state. Although the full faith and credit principles of the U.S. Constitution should permit a document properly drafted in your home state to be honored in other states, it makes sense to reduce the chance that a healthcare provider could challenge the legality of a directive based on a technicality.

Where to Keep Your Healthcare Proxies

It is important to understand that healthcare proxies are only useful if they are available to your agents and healthcare providers in a medical emergency. You should provide a copy to each agent you have named and to your doctors. You should also have one readily available for yourself, particularly if you travel.

For a small subscription fee, you can file your proxies with a repository company and your forms can be available via fax to healthcare providers worldwide, 24 hours a day and seven days a week. The repository gives you a wallet card to keep with your insurance card. The wallet card has instructions on how to obtain the forms. See *www.mypersonalwishes.com* or your legal advisor for more information on services of this kind.

Guardianship

During a period of mental incapacity someone must pay your bills and make financial decisions to take care of you, your family, your pets and attend to your other obligations. If you have bank accounts titled jointly with another person, the joint owner can continue to use those accounts. However, if only your name appears on your accounts, your financial power of attorney agents will be required to show proof of their authority to act.

If you don't have the proper legal directives or if they don't cover a particular situation, your loved ones might need to get a court order granting legal authority to act on your behalf now that you are mentally incapacitated. The process of getting this authority is called a "guardianship" proceeding and is controlled by the state probate laws. This is why it is sometimes referred to as "living probate"—the probate laws apply while you are living.

Guardianship proceedings involve three factors: *1)* Determination of mental incapacity; *2)* Giving of authority over the ward's personal affairs and/or the ward's financial affairs; and *3)* Accounting to the court regarding the guardian's actions as they pertain to the ward's financial affairs.

First, guardianship requires that you produce medical evidence of the person's mental incapacity. The statute will normally require that the level of proof required to prove that a person has lost his mental capacity be "clear and convincing" evidence or some other appropriate standard. The courts are reluctant to take away a person's autonomy. Therefore, the level of proof is sufficiently high to confine court intervention to serious situations.

Second, the court will determine who should be appointed the guardian of the incapacitated person. The hierarchy of candidates for guardians is governed by statute. You can nominate a guardian for yourself as discussed below but the court is not bound by this nomination.

The court might divide the authority "over the person" and "over the estate or property" of the incapacitated ward. This means that a family member might be named as the guardian over the physical well-being of the ward but an accountant or professional guardian might be named to handle the financial affairs. This is likely to occur where the court has some concern that a family member lacks sophistication or is at risk to exploit the ward or be exploited if placed in charge of the ward's finances.

Third, regular accounting reports must be given to the court to permit it to supervise the guardian's activities. Expenditures from the ward's assets must comply with specific standards and the court will review all accounts on a regular basis—usually bi-annually or annually. Failure to comply with the standards required by the court can be grounds for removal of the guardian.

The guardian can normally receive reasonable compensation for handling the ward's affairs. Non-family members who are named as guardians are usually required to secure a bond (like an insurance policy) to cover losses to the ward's financial accounts due the guardian's fault or neglect.

If the ward regains mental capacity, the ward will need to produce medical proof of this fact and convince the court to return authority to the ward to handle his or her affairs.

Pre-Need Guardian Declaration Directive

A pre-need guardian declaration is a directive that states your preference for the selection of a guardian of the person or guardian of the property in the event your disability directives are ineffective or absent and there is an incapacity proceeding to determine your capacity. State statutes will generally favor family members over friends or companions unless you make your selection known. A pre-need guardian directive is normally what we refer to as "a sweater in a suitcase." You don't generally need it at the time it is created, but like that extra sweater you pack when you take a trip where the weather can be uncertain, it sure is nice to have it if it becomes necessary. The pre-need guardian declaration stands by and is not used unless and until there is a guardianship proceeding pending.

Other General Issues Regarding Disability

In the event of a disability, unmarried individuals face a number of hurdles that may not be present for their married counterparts. Spouses always have a preference as healthcare surrogates and agents, and as guardians. The rules for applying for and receiving disability compensation favor married couples. A live-in friend or companion cannot make a disability claim utilizing your earning history as is possible with a spouse. Therefore, it is important if you have friends or companions that rely upon you for support to make specific financial plans and arrangements to address the concerns that may arise in the event you become disabled and are not able to work. The same is true after retirement or if you have to enter a nursing home—the rules do not necessarily favor unmarried individuals. For any type of government eligibility program, the rules for unmarried individuals are inevitably the rules that apply to single individuals. In some instances, this can be an advantage or it can be a disadvantage. If you live in a spousal support state, marriage may actually be a disadvantage if one party needs to qualify for Medicaid but the family assets exceed the limitations for eligibility.

Trusts—Financial and Healthcare Directives on Steroids

The prior sections illustrate the potential dangers that may be faced when a family member becomes mentally incapacitated. This is particularly important since insurance statistics show that we have a greater likelihood of becoming disabled at a young age than of dying prematurely.

Trusts are normally discussed in terms of "death planning" and Chapter 4 explains many of the advantages of trusts for avoiding threats to our loved ones and their financial support when we die. Often, what is not discussed is the power trusts offer in the context of disability planning.

Well-designed trusts have the potential to permit you to avoid guardianship proceedings, to keep your healthcare and financial matters private, and to permit you to name those you love and have confidence in to manage your affairs for you when you cannot do so for yourself. For unmarried individuals this can be of particular concern because of the inherent biases favoring next of kin over friends or companions regarding health and financial powers of attorney.

A trust can allow you the flexibility of naming a friend, companion or others you trust to a disability panel to determine if and when you are mentally incapacitated. For this concept to make sense, you have to think about the process. There are a couple of ways a person can be declared mentally disabled. One way is a voluntary designation of disability. One morning you wake up, decide you are no longer capable of managing your own financial affairs and making your own healthcare decisions, and you resign as trustee of your trust in favor of your designated successor trustee. Easy to say, harder to do in practice. It is the rare individual who recognizes he or she no longer has the mental capacity to make their own decisions. Rather, the reality is that most people who have lost their mental faculties have no idea they are not operating on all cylinders and proceed through life as if everything is fine.

This is where the creation and selection of a disability panel, empowered under the terms of a trust, becomes important. It is your opportunity to construct a panel of individuals you trust to make difficult decisions regarding your mental capacity. Therefore, it is critical that, at a time when you are actually going to be in disagreement with these people, you trust their judgment enough to make this difficult decision for you.

Generally, it is recommended you consider some combination of both medical professionals and family or friends to serve on this panel. You should include someone from the medical community to make sure you are getting a competent evaluation of all the factors that might result in a mental disability determination. Typically, one medical representative may include your primary care physician— generally defined as the doctor who maintains custody of your permanent medical records—and a specialist recommended by your primary care physician and approved by your spouse, trusted family member or close friend. In these days of HMOs some people do not feel comfortable naming their primary care physician as part of their disability panel because they don't feel they enjoy the type of close, personal relationship with this person that will allow the doctor to make an informed decision. You may want to carefully consider whether naming your primary care physician adds complexity to the disability determination process or provides an element of protection.

The specialist on your panel could be a doctor specializing in the type of mental incapacity you are suffering from. Therefore, the exact identity of this person may not be known, but a description as to the type of physician is included in the trust to ensure their participation on the disability panel. You can instruct that the primary care physician select a physician of appropriate medical specialty and give the right to approve the selection to your spouse, other trusted family member or close friend. This gives your family or friends a measure of control to determine the medical component that will comprise your disability panel.

There is no limit to the number of individuals you can place on your panel but carefully consider the possible result when too many committee members are trying to make a decision. After the disability panel members and appropriate alternates have been identified, it is also important to consider whether their decision should be unanimous or a majority decision. There are no right or wrong answers. As always, you have to balance the complexity of the process with the protection it may provide to you.

The panel's sole responsibility is to decide if you are mentally incapacitated. Once the panel makes a finding of mental incapacity, it plays no role unless it is asked to determine whether you have regained capacity at some point in the future. This is important because the person serving on the disability panel is not responsible for the management of your assets. The dual role of serving on your disability panel and acting as a successor trustee would only occur if you selected that individual to serve in both functions.

Once the disability determination has been made, an individual, group of individuals or corporate trustee that you select assumes management responsibility for the trust and must manage the trust assets in the role of "disability trustee." As mentioned above, if your named successor is an individual or individuals, they might be the same people you named to be on your disability panel. As a disability trustee, the scope of their responsibility includes managing the trust assets for the benefit of the beneficiary—you—and anyone else you may authorize, according to the instructions you provide in the trust document.

The instructions you provide in your trust for the management of your finances and your personal care during mental disability are very important. In fact, these may be some of the most important instructions you leave. Generally, boilerplate type trusts simply say that, "if two doctors determine the trustmaker is mentally incapacitated, then the successor trustee(s) shall take over the management of the assets." That is the extent of the instructions. As in Maggie's case, rarely are boilerplate instructions complete as to how this day-to-day management is to be accomplished. Therefore, your trust instructions need to be complete, comprehensive and specific with regard to how your assets may be spent on your behalf or on behalf of your loved ones (including your pets) when you are no longer directing the actual distribution of assets.

You will want to consider crafting instructions that specifically identify the individuals, including yourself, who may benefit from the trust assets during disability. These individuals might include your spouse, a partner or companion, your children, other family members who may be dependent upon you for their support, such as parents, siblings or friends and last but not least, your pets.

In addition, you should create excellent instructions regarding your living conditions, lifestyle, access to friends, family and pets and your specific likes and dislikes regarding your continuing care. Remember, these instructions need to be crafted while you are competent because you may not be able to communicate your wishes and desires regarding your care during a period of mental disability.

Our friend, Maggie Kinnick, could have benefited considerably if she had been advised to take the time to create disability instructions so that she could live out her life in a style that was consistent with her likes, preferences and financial ability to pay.

Summary

Our personal living trusts give instructions that state we would prefer to remain in our homes during any period of mental disability, and only if it becomes impractical or impossible for us to stay in our homes should our spouses, partners or families consider an alternate living arrangement. In the event we must live somewhere other than our home, it is our desire that we live in a place that is consistent with our maximum degree of independence. For both of us, this includes an environment that is pet-friendly and willing to accept at least one, if not all, of our small cats and dogs. It is unlikely we could find a place that would accept horses, but... In addition, our trusts provide that our successor disability trustees can spend all of our assets, if necessary, to provide for the level of care we have dictated. We have also included language to instruct our successor trustee to look for more detailed hand-written instructions with regard to our personal preferences for daily care, such as hair color, make-up, special treats and our own peculiarities. Our successor trustees are also instructed not to pay for care inconsistent with our living will and to seek guidance from our written memorial instructions in the event we die and such arrangements become necessary.

When all is said and done, if you don't leave good disability instructions, your successor disability trustees will not be provided with guidance in order to give you the type of continuing care you desire. Becoming mentally disabled should not sentence a person to a lifestyle that is inconsistent with their life prior to the onset of the disability. Be sure to make disability planning a priority in your life.

If you choose not to prepare a living trust and instead intend to rely on your last will and testament as your final expression of your wishes in the event of your death, it is wise to ensure that your estate plan include a better-than-average durable financial power of attorney, durable healthcare power of attorney, living will, anatomical gift declaration and pre-need guardian declaration. Each of these planning directives meets a different need but all are important to a well-rounded, comprehensive disability plan. In addition, handwritten instructions regarding your requirements for care in the event of disability will be one of the best defenses against being warehoused as opposed to living a quality existence.

The specifics of the decisions we need to make when planning for what happens when we die are discussed in depth in the next chapter.

Chapter 4

Planning for Your Death

What Happens When You Die?

Married or unmarried, three things occur when you die: *1)* Final arrangements for your physical remains are completed; *2)* Your estate is settled or administered; and *3)* Your loved ones and friends carry on life without you. The legacy you leave for them will consist of more than just tangible things. If you plan ahead with appropriate legal directives to authorize your final wishes and estate matters, the unintended outcomes your loved ones might face with legal issues will be reduced. If you fail to plan ahead, your loved ones can be the unfortunate victims of legal processes that dictate outcomes you would not choose for them.

A long-standing statistic reveals that more than half the population (married or unmarried) does not even have basic wills or other legal directives in place to direct their affairs at death. More than half of this segment have advanced education degrees which means that even educated people have failed to protect themselves with basic estate planning directives.

Some statistics report that out of those who do have wills, more than 40% of those wills are ten years old or older. As discussed in prior chapters, if you die without a will state laws will dictate what your loved ones are entitled to receive. If your will is old and out-of-date when you die, it may not accurately reflect your wishes. Still, your personal representative will be required to follow the out-of-date written instructions you have left behind.

The survivor of a married couple has many legal protections when the spouse dies—even when a deceased spouse failed to execute appropriate legal directives. Unmarried individuals do not enjoy the same legal protections and surviving partners are particularly vulnerable to bad outcomes if they fail to do planning. Planning and preparing legal directives are the only solutions to avoid potential problems.

We all need to plan for the time when we will die. We may not like to think about death, talk about death or accept that death is a reality, but without planning we are left with only the rules and provisions provided by our individual states. Rarely do these state rules reflect our true hopes, dreams and aspirations for our loved ones.

Some of the planning areas, in addition to legal directives, that require our attention are detailed below.

Final Arrangements

A topic that doesn't receive much attention in most discussions on estate planning is what to do with the deceased person's remains. Some states have statutes that provide for who has priority to make these decisions if the deceased person has failed to make arrangements. Surviving spouses and next of kin have priority on this list. Unmarried partners or companions are not on the list. This means that, in the eyes of the law, family members will have greater priority than the surviving partner of an unmarried person even if the family has been estranged from the deceased. If the family and surviving partner disagree, the law could legitimately support the family over the surviving partner regarding the remains and their disposition. Today, even our soldiers are being required to designate someone to handle the disposition of their remains.

Regardless of your marital status, you can and should make written instructions setting forth your wishes for disposition of your remains when you die. Your instructions regarding disposition of your remains and funeral arrangements should set forth your wishes on the following:

- Cremation, burial or donation to science
- If you want a funeral or memorial service include details as to whether you want a viewing; the type and cost of a casket; flowers or donations to charities in lieu of flowers
- Religious or other type of service; whether you want special music or a reading you would like included in the service
- Obituary, or death notices including how you want your family members and loved ones listed as survivors
- Any other details, including parting words, you would like to include regarding your final arrangements

Your memorial letter of instruction is called a "precatory" letter and is not binding, but will provide guidance to your family, loved ones and others, including successor trustees if you have a trust. If you have concerns that your wishes might not be followed, either due to financial reasons or because family members share a different vision of how you should be laid to rest, consider making pre-paid funeral arrangements. Pre-paid funerals can include every detail you want for your final arrangements. Family members and loved ones are less likely to dispute arrangements if they don't bear the financial responsibility for them.

Pre-paid funeral arrangements will be especially important for people who have selected a corporate trustee to succeed them in the event of disability or death and will insure that you will have the type of service and arrangements you desire. However, be aware that most pre-paid plans are not transferable to other states if you move. You should thoroughly explore your options and have the contract for funeral services reviewed by a legal professional.

A carefully detailed set of instructions regarding your final arrangements is one of the greatest gifts you can give to your survivors. They are relieved of the burden of guessing what you would want and only need to follow the instructions you have left.

When one of our clients died, his memorial plans were so well documented and detailed that even the priest that conducted the service commented that he didn't know whether he should make any comments of his own. The client wrote down who should officiate, who should be invited to attend, who should read each part of the service, that he wanted to be cremated and what the family should do with the remains after the service. Years later, the family still recounts with pride, love and affection, the care their father took to relieve them of this responsibility at a significant time of grief.

If you decide not to make pre-paid funeral arrangements, you should have some idea about how your final arrangements will be paid. Insurance is the traditional mechanism most people use to cover funeral costs, and it is sometimes available through your employer as a work-related benefit. Some insurance companies offer burial plans that provide just enough insurance to pay for final expenses. In some cases, no medical examination process is required to obtain this type of insurance.

Administering Your Estate

Passing on Your 'Stuff' To Others When You are Gone

As the old saying goes, "You can't take it with you." When you die, the "stuff" you own gets passed on to survivors. The generic term for this process is "estate settlement" or "estate administration." When an estate is settled, title to your stuff is transferred to others in basically three ways:
- Probate
- Operation of law
- Contract

The method of transfer and the consequences of the transfer depend on a number of factors. These factors include:
- How title to assets is held

- What legal directives are in place to direct the assets at death
- The total value of the deceased person's estate

Unmarried partners have special considerations in addition to the above factors:
- The amount(s) each partner contributed to acquire the asset
- The amount(s) each partner gave to others during life (in other words, the total gifts they made during their lifetimes)

An effective estate plan will coordinate the above factors with your specific needs and goals. Obviously, boilerplate and do-it-yourself wills and other legal directives carry the potential for producing a poor result if you do not understand how they work in the whole scheme of things.

Title Controls

How title to assets is held and how title affects transfers of assets is one of the most misunderstood areas for non-lawyers facing estate planning decisions. Few people realize the legal consequences associated with how they hold title. They don't realize that every time they open a bank or brokerage account, complete a beneficiary designation form or execute a deed, they are engaging in estate planning, of sorts. They also don't realize that a will or a trust will be powerless to direct an asset if they own it as joint tenants with rights of survivorship (JTROS or JTWROS) with another person.

Estate planning involves coordinating your categories of asset ownership with your legal directives, consistent with your overall estate planning goals. Consequently, it is important to understand the different categories of title, and that each specific category of title controls which mechanism is used to transfer assets at death. Without this understanding, you might not have the proper types of legal directives to achieve your goals. Your estate planning goals can be anything from minimizing the delay and expense of administration to reducing or avoiding estate taxes to avoiding probate or providing asset protection for survivors. These are just a few worthy estate planning objectives and there are others equally as important.

The basic rules regarding how assets are transferred are the same for both married and unmarried couples. It is just that state laws build in legal safety nets for married partners and their children to make sure they are not accidentally disinherited. Unmarried partners have no automatic legal safety nets. Therefore, it is essential that unmarried partners create their own safety nets to ensure that their wishes will be followed.

Understanding the rules that control transfers at death is easiest if you remember that each category of ownership must have an "instruction sheet" to direct the asset at the owner's death. Some assets have built-in instructions as to who gets the asset at the owner's death, such as with a payable on death account or a jointly owned property. Other categories of assets rely on a person's will for instructions as to who gets the asset, such as investments held in an individual's name.

The chart at the end of Appendix "B" illustrates the interplay between how title is held and transferred at an owner's death. A detailed explanation of this interplay follows.

Probate

Probate is a state-authorized court process to settle the deceased person's final debts and to formally pass legal title to property from the deceased person's name to others. A will is the instruction sheet for property titled in a person's individual name. The instructions in the will tell the court who should get the property. If there is no will, or if it is invalid for some reason, probate is still required for property held in the individual's name. However, the court must follow the instructions under state probate laws for people who have died without a will. These laws are called intestate succession or intestacy rules.

A person who makes a will is called the testator or testatrix. A person who does not have a valid will is said to have died intestate.

Intestate succession is the term to describe the state probate laws list of next-of-kin who stand in line to receive probate property where the deceased died without a valid will.

The probate process only controls property in a person's individual name. The probate process does not control property that has a built in survivorship feature, such as joint tenants with survivorship rights property, property with beneficiary designations or property that has been titled into the name of a trust. However, if there is a flaw in any of these ownership categories, your heirs will have to resort to the probate process to get title passed because the original "instructions" for that asset can no longer be followed. It is also important to note that there are forms of joint ownership that do not have built-in survivorship language, such as tenants in common.

Most states have special probate rules for smaller estates that streamline the time frames and process to keep the probate costs to a minimum. These rules often have names, such as "release from administration" or "small estate probate."

The probate process essentially involves three steps:
1) Identify and gather all of the decedent's assets that are owned in the decedent's individual name.
2) Identify and pay all of the decedent's creditors, including taxes, within a time frame set by law.
3) Identify the beneficiaries and distribute the probate assets accordingly, either by looking at the names or categories of relatives set forth in the will or by looking to the "no will" rules of intestate succession.

The term "probate estate" refers to the assets that are controlled by the probate process under a will or the "no will" probate of intestate succession. The probate estate will not include property that does not require the probate process to pass title to others. This means the probate estate will not include a car or parcel of real estate that has title under a "transfer on death" deed or title. The probate estate is not the same thing as the taxable estate for estate tax purposes.

There are some disadvantages of probate you should consider when making estate planning decisions and creating your legal directives:

- Probate is a public proceeding. This means the nature and extent of the probate assets can be scrutinized by anyone who cares to look up the record at the court. This is easier to do these days since most courts have case documents available on-line through the internet.

- The probate process requires filing fees, legal costs, appraiser fees for real estate and special types of assets, and accounting fees. These fees can add up to sizeable amounts on larger estates. (Note: some or most of these fees may be required even if probate is avoided.)

- If a trust is created in the will, called a "testamentary trust," there may be additional costs to the estate for the ongoing administration of these trusts pursuant to the instructions in the will.

- The probate process can be lengthy, depending on the nature of the probate assets. Beneficiaries under the will generally do not gain access to the assets while the process is pending. However, most state's probate laws give surviving spouses access to limited sums to live on during the probate process. There is currently no comparable provision for unmarried partners to receive a similar family allowance. Unmarried partners are treated no differently than single beneficiaries in the eyes of the law.

- Disgruntled heirs (blood relatives) can challenge a will before the probate judge and, perhaps, change some of the distributions set forth in the will if the judge rules in their favor.

The probate process has advantages as well:

- The decedent's creditors have to present their claims to the decedent's estate within specified time frames or forego payment. In addition, the personal representative can dispute a suspect claim and the court will decide if the claim is valid.

- Another advantage is, ironically, one of its disadvantages—the fact that the process is public. This means that the process and details of the estate are subject to scrutiny by others, a fact that may make mishandling of probate estate assets more difficult and easier to detect than in a private administration process.

- Finally, the fact that it is a court-supervised process means that the process must follow known procedures that can impose a degree of orderliness and predictability.

Even if it is your intent to avoid probate by owning assets with built-in survivorship features, it is always a good idea to have a will in place anyway. Wills can act as a safety net if there is a defect in one of the non-probate transfer mechanisms or if you die with an unexpected asset in your name. This could occur, for instance, if you receive an inheritance from a family member and die shortly thereafter or if you bought the winning lottery ticket but didn't have time to deposit the proceeds into your account.

A will controls these individually owned assets and the survivors avoid having to go through probate under the intestate succession rules which might distribute the assets differently than you desired. Remember, the "pecking order" set forth in the intestate succession rules in most states don't always give your property to the people you want at your death.

Wills

Wills must be executed with certain legal formalities to be considered valid. Each state decides its own standards about what formalities must be followed. In general, most states require that the maker of a will have legal capacity (be mentally competent), be of legal age (at least eighteen years old), and that the execution of the will was of the maker's free and intentional act. You must follow the rules of the state in which you reside at the time the will is executed.

Most states require that the will be written and signed by the maker of the will before one or more witnesses. Handwritten wills, called holographic wills, are permitted in many states and may not need to be witnessed but must meet other standards to be considered valid. Each state will have its own requirements for a holographic will to be considered valid. We know of one instance where a will that was written on a piece of notebook paper in the hospital and properly witnessed was validly admitted for probate purposes. Do-it-yourself holographic wills are generally not recommended, however.

A detailed discussion of the requirements for executing a will is beyond the scope of this book. However, it is important to note that unmarried partners should consult an attorney to have their wills prepared in order to be confident that the will meets the standards required in their state. It is fool-hardy for most married couples to do a home-made will, but at least they have the intestate rules that are better than nothing.

Wills don't have to follow a particular format, but they usually do. The first paragraph normally recites the essential elements about the maker of the will being of legal age and sound mind, and how the making of the will was the maker's own free act. The next paragraph normally authorizes payment of the maker's debts and the costs of administrating the probate estate and taxes from the estate. The next paragraph may direct the distribution of specific personal property, followed by a paragraph that directs the remainder of the estate to whomever the maker wants. This is normally referred to as the "residuary estate" clause because it directs the distribution of the balance of the estate (the residuary) after paying taxes and debts.

The will should nominate someone to act as the personal representative of the estate. This person is normally called the executor (male) or executrix (female) and the nomination clause can specify whether the personal representative must post a bond and whether they are entitled to collect a fee for performing their duties as the personal representative. A bond is like an insurance policy to protect the estate from losses caused by the personal representative if they fail to properly carry out their duties.

If you have minor children, the will nominates those individuals you choose as guardians for their care. These individuals should be people you trust and that have your same or similar values. These will be the people that may end up with the responsibility of raising your children in the event you are unable. This one decision is often the road block that prevents couples with children from doing their planning. The couple can't agree on the choice of guardian and somehow reconcile that not making the decision is better than facing an on-going argument. This results in a default decision whereby the guardianship of their children is left to chance, statute and the whims of the court system. We have always believed that a decision by design is always better than a decision by default. We sometimes tell our clients that they don't have to agree, each parent can choose their own set of guardians for the children. The issue then becomes which of the parents will live the longest and have their wishes honored. In addition to naming the guardians for minor children in a will, it is important to leave detailed written instructions regarding how you want your children raised. These instructions are similar to the "baby-sitter" instructions you leave when you go out for a couple of hours, only now the instructions are essential for the care of your children if you never return. These instructions should include all of your hopes, dreams and aspirations for your children.

The will can create a trust to hold the minor children's assets for their benefit until they reach the age of majority or some other specified age. This is different than a revocable living trust (RLT) because a RLT is not created under a will and, consequently, does not go through probate. More information about RLTs will be provided later in this chapter.

Operation Of Law

States can create categories of property ownership that, by the terms of the state law, automatically give ownership of the property to the surviving owners at the death of the original owner. These categories of ownership can be created by the common law of a state or can be created under state statute or code. For example, tenancy by the entirety (TBE) is a type of survivorship ownership that is limited to married couples. Probate is not required to determine who receives the property at the owner's death because the instructions are built into the type of ownership itself.

Assets Held Jointly With Others

People can own assets with others as tenants in common (TIC) and as joint tenants with rights of survivorship (JTROS or JTWROS). Most people prefer the JTROS form of ownership but sometimes make a mistake, and do not include the required "survivorship" language when executing a deed. Therefore, they think they have JTROS when they actually have created TIC ownership. The difference determines whether they need probate to pass title at death, among other things.

Tenants in Common (TIC)

A person's interest in a TIC asset is controlled by a person's will since they own a specified percentage of the asset and can convey that percentage interest to others during life and at death. The beneficiary(ies) under the will, or the heir(s) under the intestate succession rules if there is no will, become the joint owner of the asset with the other joint owners. There is no built-in survivorship language in a TIC owned asset. The surviving owners do not get the deceased person's share unless they were named as a beneficiary in the will or they are a natural heir if there is no will. This means that survivors can end up owning property with the deceased person's heirs— something they may or may not have contemplated when they acquired the property as TIC originally.

Joint Tenants with Rights of Survivorship (JTROS or JTWROS)

This form of property ownership is probably one of the most common examples of the operation of law principles. It is a popular

form of ownership because it is easy and inexpensive to create. Many people choose this type of ownership because it avoids probate and appears to create a fair division of assets between couples, married or not. For many unmarried partners, it symbolizes their commitment and seems to protect their mutual interests in each other's property. However, these so-called advantages can obscure some of the less desirable qualities of JTROS, such as:

- The asset is available to the creditors of all joint owners.
- A taxable gift can be triggered if unmarried owners contribute unequal amounts to the cost of acquiring the asset.
- The entire value of the asset will be included in the estate (for purposes of calculating the federal estate tax) of the first owner to die unless the survivor can produce proof of his or her contributions to the property or other proof as to why less than the full amount should be included.
- Structuring financial accounts as JTROS makes the account available to all joint owners and any owner can legally withdraw all of the account funds without the permission of the other owners.
- There can be income tax consequences associated with JTROS property involving capital gains on the property. The most recent federal estate tax laws have modified the rules on step-up in basis at death, and there is some debate whether these rules will remain in place. Therefore, it will be important for a couple, married or unmarried, to consult with appropriate advisors if their assets are sizeable to be sure they understand the tax consequences of transferring their estates at death.
- A joint owner requires consent of the other owner to sell real property held as JTROS during life (this can be a good thing as well— read the section on disadvantages for contract assets below).
- There is no mechanism to hold JTROS property in trust for the benefit of a disabled surviving owner. If the surviving owner is in a nursing home at the time the other owner passes away, the value of the property might make the survivor ineligible for needs-based public benefits.

- JTROS does not work well in the event of the simultaneous deaths of owners since the property will be included in the estates of both and will require that the asset go through probate.

Federal and state estate taxes might be due at the death of the first owner and the estate might not have sufficient liquid assets to cover them. In addition to gift and estate tax consequences, if an owner, either married or unmarried, is not a U.S. citizen the rules for gift and inheritance taxes may vary. In some states, there may also be a state inheritance or estate tax at the time of death.

Once the property is transferred to the survivor at the death of the first owner, the surviving owner can direct who gets the asset thereafter regardless of the original understanding of the joint owners. Therefore, there is no guarantee the property will go to the people originally agreed upon between the partners.

Transfer on Death Deeds (TOD) or Deeds with a Retained Life Estate or Remainder

These deeds to real estate are individually owned titles with a survivorship or remainder feature. The asset remains in the individual name of the owner but it is not controlled by a will or the probate process because the deed has a built-in survivorship provision that directs who gets the property at the owner's death.

This type of deed is easy to create and inexpensive. The survivor merely produces proof of the death of the owner, and an affidavit is generally filed with the county recorder's office to create a paper trail showing how and why title was transferred.

TOD assets do not have all of the disadvantages that JTROS property have in terms of potential gift tax issues or being subject to a joint owner's control or creditor's control. Some disadvantages of TOD are as follows:
- The entire value of the asset is included in the deceased owner's gross estate for purposes of calculating the federal and state estate tax.

- If estate taxes are due at the death of the first owner, the estate might not have sufficient liquid assets to pay them.
- The asset is available to the owner's creditors during life (but not available to the survivor's creditors until the survivor receives the property in his or her own name at the death of the owner).
- There is no mechanism to hold the asset for the benefit of a disabled survivor.
- The survivor decides who gets the asset once it is transferred to the survivor's name regardless of what the original owner and the survivor had discussed prior to the original owner's death.
- They are not available in every state.

Contractual Property Rights

Many of us have contracts that entitle us to direct benefits to survivors at our deaths. Some of these contracts are associated with employee benefits at work. The most common examples of assets transferring via contract are insurance policies, retirement accounts, annuities and payable-on-death accounts (POD).

POD provisions might appear to be the same as transfer-on-death deeds. They are not technically the same since they do not get their legal standing from state law but get it from contract provisions offered by financial institutions. Therefore, they belong in the family of assets that transfer via contract provisions rather than by operation of law.

Trusts are technically part of this category, but will be discussed separately because of their unique features. Trusts can be drafted to overcome many of the disadvantages of any other form of ownership and can also provide disability planning for the owner if well-drafted.

The terms of the POD contract permit the owner to identify who receives the property under the contract when the owner dies. The owner must complete a beneficiary designation form identifying the beneficiary. The beneficiary designation form is the instruction sheet for the proceeds controlled by the contract.

A will has no power over the contract proceeds and will not direct who gets the benefits under the contract. The only exception to this rule is if the beneficiary form is defective for some reason or if the named beneficiary(ies) dies before the owner dies and there is no one else named to take the benefit under the contract, or if the owner names their estate as the beneficiary. In these situations, the contract would have an owner (who is deceased) but no named beneficiary. Therefore, probate will be needed to direct who gets the benefit.

Contract assets have some of the advantages of the other ownership methods discussed above:

- There is no need for probate unless there is a problem with the beneficiary designation.
- There are no costs associated with creating the beneficiary designation.
- The transfer process is private and is not part of a court record.
- Some benefits are not considered income to the beneficiary so no income tax is due upon receipt.
- In most cases, a trust can be named as a beneficiary to avoid issues associated with outright distributions.

Some disadvantages of contract assets are:

- With some exceptions, the asset is available to the owner's creditors during life and may have been exhausted before the owner dies.
- The asset can be included in the deceased owner's estate for purposes of calculating the federal and state gross taxable estate.
- There is no mechanism for holding the asset for the survivor's benefit if the survivor is a minor or is disabled at the time of the transfer.
- The ability to continue income tax deferral during the balance of the survivor's lifetime is not available for unmarried partners as it is for married partners.
- An unmarried owner can change the beneficiary any time prior to death or incapacity without the consent of the survivor, which can be a good thing or a bad thing. Some states prevent married couples from changing the beneficiary from the spouse without the spouse's written consent, as a protection against being disinherited.

Trusts

People can create trusts to address their unique needs. They can have more than one type of trust, depending on their particular circumstances. Trusts can be what we call "living" trusts or "testamentary" trusts. They can be revocable or irrevocable. An explanation of these terms is below.

A trust only controls property that is held in the name of the trust. The process of changing the title of assets into the name of the trust is called "funding" or asset integration. Assets held in an individual's name or as joint tenants with rights of survivorship are not controlled by the trust terms.

A revocable living trust (RLT) is in effect when it is signed—when you are living. These are also called *inter vivos* trusts, which is the Latin term meaning "between the living." The provisions in these trusts can include instructions and legal authority for taking care of the trustmaker and loved ones during the trustmaker's life while he or she is alive and well or in the event of their disability. A trust can also provide authority to support a trustmaker's beneficiaries at the trustmaker's death.

Testamentary trusts are trusts that are created in a will. They do not exist until the maker of the will dies and the will is administered (probated). Therefore, unlike living trusts, testamentary trusts must go through the probate process. Because a testamentary trust cannot come into existence until the maker of the will dies and the will that created the testamentary trusts is probated, a testamentary trust cannot provide instructions to take care of the maker or his or her loved ones during a period of disability in the maker's life.

Revocable trusts and testamentary trusts created in a will can be modified anytime up to the time the maker dies or becomes incompetent. In a revocable trust, the trustmaker can authorize others to modify the trust terms even when the trustmaker is incompetent or has died. The agent in the trust who is authorized to make changes is generally referred to as a "trust protector."

Irrevocable trusts are created during the trustmaker's lifetime but they generally cannot be amended after creation except by court order or under other limited conditions.

There are many benefits of trusts. Some of the most commonly cited advantages are:

- Trust terms are private since they do not require the public probate process.
- Assets can be divided into sub-trusts to permit the trustmaker to take advantage of tax planning rules while still taking care of survivors. These sub-trusts are commonly referred to as A-B trusts or marital and family trusts. A detailed explanation of this mechanism is beyond the scope of this book but more information can be found in Chapter 8—Taxation.
- A trust can hold assets for the benefit of a named beneficiary rather than placing the asset directly into the name of the beneficiary. This protects the asset from being vulnerable to the beneficiary's creditors or to waste caused by the beneficiary.
- A trust can hold assets for a beneficiary's use during the beneficiary's lifetime, with the balance of the assets passing to others (perhaps children from a prior relationship or grandchildren) at the beneficiary's death.
- Trust terms can be drafted to enhance the likelihood that payments from the trust supplement rather than supplant a beneficiary's needs-based public disability benefits, if any.
- If properly drafted, trusts can provide a way to manage assets while the survivor is coping with the grieving process.
- The mechanisms for contesting a trust are more difficult than for wills.

Summary Regarding Ownership of Assets

This discussion of title should illustrate that it is essential that you understand the category into which your assets fall and make sure the categories are consistent with your overall wishes for distributing

your assets at death and other estate planning goals. You should make sure you have the appropriate legal directives in place to control your assets.

Whether your assets are mostly TOD, POD, held in trust or individually owned, you should have a basic understanding of what each type of ownership represents and how each directive can meet your needs and accomplish your goals, as well as how your goals can be thwarted if your circumstances change after you execute the directives.

This discussion of title and Maggie's story should underscore that title is not the end-all of estate planning for the directives and guidance you need to provide for your own care and that of your survivors when you are not available to do so. Your directives need to provide sufficient personal instructions with legal authority to permit your survivors and caretakers to understand how your assets are to be used.

Remember, the people empowered to handle Maggie's affairs were not inherently evil or devious. They were probably conservative business people who were carrying our their duties within the strict letter of the law. Maggie had the appropriate legal directives in place to control the trust assets. She just did not have sufficient personal instructions and guidance in place to get more than a generic treatment of her needs and administration of her assets.

Ask your advisors about how your directives will play out in "what if" scenarios that apply to your personal and financial situation. This will help you decide where you need to give greater personalized guidance to those who will attempt to follow your written instructions.

Chapter 5

The Importance of Personal Instructions

It is our desire that in writing this book we will impress upon you the importance of leaving well-written, well-conceived directives that are both legally and technically correct. However, it may be even more important to leave more personalized instructions that detail your wishes with regard to your disability or death. Any competent law firm can assist your loved ones in carrying out the legal directives. Only you can provide proper instructions for your day-to-day care and the special instructions that may make the difference between existing and really living.

A few years ago we found a book by Erin Tierney Kramp called *Living with the End in Mind—a Practical Checklist for Living Life to the Fullest by Embracing Your Mortality*. This book was written by a woman, also a mother, who knew she was dying of a terminal illness. She used her remaining time to create a legacy for her only daughter. In addition to the book, she wrote letters, made video tapes and other recordings so that she could continue to influence her daughter's life even when she was no longer going to be physically present. We were touched by her genuine concern for her daughter and for her depth of understanding that leaving a living legacy is more important that the *things* we leave behind. We believe that life is enriched when we come to fully understand and appreciate that what's really important in life is not the things—but the people that have affected our lives.

Personal Letters and Ethical Wills

There are an unlimited number of ways you can leave personal instructions for your family. A letter is probably the easiest to physically create yet the hardest emotionally. One of our friends, has a letter written by his mother that is one of his most cherished possessions. She died when he was thirteen—one of a number of children. Yet here again, we have a mother with the foresight, concern and love for her children that she found a way to leave a permanent legacy. Our friend went on to become an estate planning attorney and has also founded an organization, Sunbridge, Inc. that is dedicated to teaching estate planning attorneys and financial advisors how to build more lasting relationships with their clients through the creation of significance in both the client and the professional's lives. As a result, we suggest everyone consider creating a Personal Legacy Declaration—essentially a letter to your family and loved ones that describes the personal legacy of the writer. It doesn't include any legal language and is not intended to transfer property— only love and values. Peggy has done this exercise personally and with both of her parents. The final result is a loving and meaningful written history of the individual's life as well as their legacy. The journey allows the individual to reflect on their personal history, the creation and impact of their values, their commitment to the world, their spirituality, as well as the depth of experience learned from life.

In the legal profession, we say it is easier to edit than create. This may be one reason why so few people take the time to create the type of written legacy that would have significance beyond any tangible gift a person can leave. Samples of personal legacy statements aren't usually provided by the majority of estate planning attorneys or advisors. For this reason, we've provided some assistance in Appendix "D" for creating your own personal legacy declaration. We hope this will give you the motivation you need to take this very important step.

If you want or need more assistance in leaving a written legacy, we encourage you to seek out a legal practitioner who will assist you in creating what some call an ethical will. It is an unusual name—it isn't really a will and we're not sure where the ethical part comes in—but it is an expression of your personal, rather than legal, desires regarding your life. Ethical wills are not legal documents but can be your true expression of the hopes, dreams, fears and desires you have for the future as well as the future of your loved ones. Ethical wills can be traced back to biblical times and can be used to tell a story, praise loved ones for the contributions to your life, make apologies—the list is endless. For more information on ethical wills, visit www.ethicalwill.com.

There is also an organization called Aging With Dignity headquartered in Tallahassee, Florida that promotes a concept known as the Five Wishes™. The Five Wishes details your desires regarding:

1) The person you want to make care decisions for you when you can't
2) The kind of medical treatment you want or don't want
3) How comfortable you want to be
4) How you want people to treat you
5) What you want your loved ones to know

The Five Wishes is designed to meet the requirements of the District of Columbia and 33 other states. For more information about the Five Wishes contact Aging With Dignity at www.agingwithdignity.org. The Five Wishes, however, is not a substitute for a living will.

Disability Instructions

Disability instructions can also be written in the form of an instruction letter. The letter doesn't need to be fancy or typed, just an expression of how you would like to be cared for if you are no longer able to care for yourself. We have often wondered if Maggie had prepared this type of written instruction whether her last years would have been lived differently? When we explain the concept of disability instructions to our clients, we suggest they think of all the little eccentricities that make them unique and then write them down on paper. Every person will have different wants and needs. Both of us want to make sure that we have the opportunity to interact with our pets as long as that is possible and thereafter, with any pet that can enrich and improve the quality of our life. In addition, Peggy would like access to her horses or other horses for the balance of her life.

Other things you may consider include, grooming requirements such as hair color, manicures, pedicures; eating habits such as food allergies, likes and dislikes, and special requests such as a happy hour beverage or favorite dessert. The list can go on and on.

Memorial Instructions

Memorial instructions are your written directives regarding your final arrangements. Do you want to be cremated or buried? Do you have a family mausoleum or burial plot? Do you want your ashes maintained or scattered? Do you have strong preferences regarding the type of memorial or service? Recently when former President Regan died, the country learned that he and Nancy Regan had crafted his final ceremony more than ten years before his death. Ronald Regan took the time and attention necessary to arrange this important detail of his life. He did not leave anything to chance. We believe this is one of the greatest gifts you can give your family because it removes a tremendous amount of pressure at a very difficult time. Imagine if all you had to do for a parent or loved one was follow a set of instructions. These instructions would not require that you make any decisions at all and you would have perfect peace knowing that you did exactly as your loved one had intended. We've included a sample Memorial Letter and Special Instructions form in Appendix "E."

The memorial instructions left by the client who detailed his entire funeral is one example of a gift of piece of mind. His family knew what to do and how to do it. They did not have to make some very difficult decisions when it was really more important that they spend their time celebrating their father's life, caring for their mother and each other. Today, the family still comments on the peace and security their father's advance instructions gave them at that time.

Personal Property Memorandum

A personal property memorandum, also affectionately known as "your special stuff list," details the distribution of your personal belongings—your stuff. This is the same stuff that George Carlin reminds us for which we have consistently purchased larger homes. It is your jewelry, furniture, collectables, antiques, sentimental items and other miscellaneous stuff to which someone may have a personal or emotional attachment.

We think the easiest way to create this list is to inventory all of your sentimental property and then make a list of each item along with the designation to whom the property should be given. Some of our clients say they intend to give away this important property during their lifetime. Of course, this is always the best way, but often we fail to get around to actually making the distributions. Some people are such collectors of stuff that they can't seem to part with any of it during their lifetime. Others are so good at down-sizing and making lifetime gifts that there is nothing left to distribute at the time of death.

One thing a personal property memorandum insures is that there is clarity about who is to receive what item. It eliminates family disagreement. It is not unusual for us to hear from a family that mom or dad "promised" an item to multiple members of the family. In fact, many family disputes center around the distribution of the sentimental items, not the more valuable items like financial assets. In addition, we've seen all matter of attempts to allow children and grandchildren to identify those items they would like to receive. One family used colored dots and each child was allotted a specific color. Then the children went around mom and dad's home and attached the colored dots to the items they would like to have. Another mother we know left instructions that each of her four children was to be given a turn to select an item from the house. Each child was to have a turn and then the turns started over again and repeated until all valuable or sentimental items in the house had been claimed. This particular family did not have great success with this method and ultimately ended up in litigation. However, some variation of this theme may work for your family.

Another idea is to have the personal property appraised and then distribute monopoly money to each of the family members and allow them to "buy" the items they would like to have. Clearly, there are a number of options for the distribution of personal property. Whichever one you choose, think through the possible good and bad outcomes so that you can create a method that will work best for your loved ones.

Personal instructions are as important, and in some cases, more important than the legal and technical directives you may leave behind. Use careful thought and preparation in the creation of your personalized instructions for your care and for the benefit of your family.

Chapter 6

Asset Integration
and Funding

It is important to keep good records regarding your assets during
your lifetime. At disability or death, family members may feel they
are playing a form of "morbid scavenger hunt" trying to determine
the identity and location of a loved one's assets and personal belongings. It is important to keep records of the following:

- Receipts for significant asset purchases. You can use an expand-
  able file for important receipts and warranty information.
- Copies of income tax returns and gift tax returns. Keep at least
  three years worth of tax returns and keep all gift tax returns.
- Originals of any legal directives including your will, trust, financial and healthcare powers of attorney, living will, pre-need
  guardian declaration, ethical will, memorial instructions, etc.
- Handwritten or other personal instructions for minor children,
  disability, death, memorial or personal property distribution.
- Location lists setting forth the location of assets and important
  papers as well as the names of advisors or others who need to be
  contacted if something should happen.
- Names and addresses of people who should be contacted in the
  event of your disability or death. Family members may not know
  all of your friends and acquaintances. We suggest keeping a copy
  of your holiday card list (computerized and updated if you have
  it) with your important documents.
- Insurance policies and copies of the beneficiary forms.
- Memorial instructions and copies of prepaid funeral contracts.

Asset Integration

Asset integration refers to the process of making sure your assets have the appropriate legal title and legal directives in order to control the management of assets during disability and distribution at death. This area of planning requires good communication between family members and your legal and financial advisors. A misstep in one area of planning can inadvertently undo a decision in another area of planning.

An error or omission regarding the title or disposition of a particular asset can cause the best legal directives to fail to achieve your goals. For instance, if you purchase life insurance as a means of creating immediate funds to support your family, naming your estate as the beneficiary will not achieve this goal. You should make sure your family gets clear instructions from your team of advisors and make sure the advisors are working in a coordinated way.

Funding Trusts

If a trust is used as the primary planning directive, the documents confirming that the trust owns the assets should be kept with the original trust. The special steps required to make sure the trust instructions control assets are set forth below.

Any trust that has no assets earmarked to fund it is essentially worthless. Steps must be undertaken to make certain the trust is funded with assets designed to meet the needs of the trustmaker during lifetime and the intended beneficiaries in the event of disability or death. "Funding a trust" means that legal title to the trustmaker's assets are changed into the name of the trust. It may also mean renaming beneficiary designations on contract assets like insurance policies, annuities and retirement plans. The ultimate objective is that all of the trustmaker's assets are either owned or ultimately controlled (through beneficiary designations) by the trust.

The creation of the legal documents for an estate plan is only the first step in the planning process. There must also be sufficient assets, properly owned, in order to make sure the instructions contained in the trust will be carried out for the ultimate benefit of the trustmaker and the beneficiaries.

It is at this stage of the planning process that the team concept of professional advisors becomes most critical. The lawyer can create the legal framework, but it is now up to you, in concert with your professional team, including a Certified Public Accountant (CPA) and other financial professionals to construct a financial plan consistent with the goals and resources that will best suit the unique needs of your family.

Transferring assets into your trust requires either a change of legal ownership of the asset during your lifetime or naming the trust as beneficiary at the death of the owner of life insurance policies, retirement plans or other beneficiary designated assets. Your advisors should be familiar with the potential tax consequences of such transfers and alert you to any potential unfavorable results. Then you can make an informed decision to accept the tax consequences, if any, or you may choose to forgo a particular solution for tax or other reasons, like asset protection.

Your financial advisor should help you make sure you have not overlooked sources of assets, such as military benefits with survivor options. Insurance has been described as a perfect mechanism for families to either create wealth or to cover the cost of taxes on wealth. Insurance can be a method to leverage smaller premium amounts in order to leave a large lump sum for the future benefit of your survivors.

The specific amount of money or assets required to adequately fund the trust for the future needs of your family members is personal to each family and requires a detailed financial plan with projections about returns on investments. Asset allocation models may need to be implemented and periodically reviewed to insure they remain consistent with long-term planning goals.

A trust can hold almost any kind of asset or can be the recipient of any kind of asset that is payable on the death of the asset owner. Although some trusts hold title to no assets until the death of the trustmaker, it is generally recommended that at least a minimum amount be placed in the trust to fund it initially.

Assets can be added to the trust over time. Additions may be made by gift during life, by will or trust, by life insurance policies, by employee plan benefits, or by retirement plan benefits.

Where to Keep Important Papers

Originals of important papers should be kept in a fireproof and waterproof box or safe. Additional consideration should be given to the type of box or safe if there is concern for theft or tampering with the contents. A fire safe box kept at home that can be carried off won't necessarily be helpful in the event of theft but could protect important papers in the event of a fire. Peggy had a client whose home was robbed and the thieves stole their fire safe box. The only thing valuable in the box was their estate planning documents, that now needed to be replaced.

Safe deposit boxes in banks are sometimes a good place to keep important papers. You will need to make individual decisions about whether to keep items in a safe deposit box and who will have authority to access the box. In some instances, it may be advisable for a revocable living trust and the corresponding trustees to be the lessees on a safe deposit box to ensure that any subsequent trustees will also have access to the box. Whether a bank safe deposit box meets the needs of you and your family depends on a number of factors.

One concern with regard to safe deposit boxes is that they may not be accessible when it is important to have immediate access to their contents. This may be especially true if you keep healthcare directives in your safe deposit box and there is a medical emergency on the weekend or on a holiday.

The long-standing rule in many states was that state law required the bank to freeze access to the box when an owner died to permit the state tax-auditing authority time to audit the safe deposit box contents. The rationale for this policy was to prevent family members from removing jewelry, negotiable instruments or other liquid assets before the tax auditors could include their value in the probate estate. Many states have relaxed the tight restraints on immediate access and permit bank officials to perform a preliminary audit of box contents after which the contents are released to an authorized person.

Sometimes there may also be concerns of family members that someone gaining early access might not share the contents of the box with others or that a will or other legal directive might be destroyed if it was not favorable to the person gaining access. The rules for intestate succession will apply if there is no will and assets were titled in the deceased's individual name or there are other types of assets but no other legal directives, such as beneficiary designations or trusts.

Some attorneys will keep the original will or other legal directives in their firm's safe or bank deposit box. Generally, this is a mechanism to enhance the likelihood that the survivors will retain the lawyer to probate the will or administer the estate. However, you need to determine what happens to the documents if the attorney becomes ill or passes away or if you lose contact with the attorney's office. Your loved ones will need to know who to contact if you haven't provided them with information about the identity of the custodian of the documents. It is not unusual to see advertisements in local bar newsletters requesting information about original wills that may be retained in the office of a local lawyer.

Many firms, however, do not retain originals, but only copies, of the documents they have prepared for the client. Therefore, the need to find a safe place for the other documents in the paper trail still must be satisfied. As a general rule, our firms do not retain original documents, unless specifically requested to do so. In addition, we advise clients to keep their documents at home in a safe but readily accessible place.

Probate courts in most jurisdictions have a repository for wills. For a small, one-time fee, a will is deposited with the court and kept confidential until the will-maker dies. At that point, the will can be admitted to probate.

If changes to the will are made, the amended or replacement wills can also be filed in the repository and cross-referencing of the filing numbers is possible. This is a way for a person to feel secure that the will can be located and submitted to the probate court at the time of their death.

If the will-maker moves to another state, decisions must be made about updating the will in the new jurisdiction and informing the first repository that the will on file is no longer current. Part of the paper trail includes clear notes when original plans have been changed. These factors should be discussed with legal advisors to arrive at the best solutions for your situation.

Family members should retain copies of their important papers with explicit instructions as to where the originals can be located. In this age of electronic records, copies on a compact disc (CD) are particularly handy for the computer literate. Obviously, some understanding of the proper storage and handling of such mechanisms is important as well.

A location list can be essential for survivors trying to recall specific locations of originals and copies of various assets. In some respects, a location list is a thoughtful gift from the deceased individual. It conveys the thought and attention the deceased had for the peace of mind and well-being of their surviving loved ones. For many of our clients, we provide a comprehensive, tabbed and organized notebook that includes pre-printed information regarding the identification of legal documents and assets that allows the will or trustmaker to further customize the list as to the exact location of many items. This notebook serves as a resource center for survivors and others as to the location of many important planning directives.

Summary

Consider creating a system for tracking both exempt and non-exempt gifts made to family members in the event of an IRS audit after death. In addition, keep good records regarding the acquisition price of all assets. This tracking system will streamline preparation of tax returns, will be useful for establishing "basis" for purposes of determining capital gains taxes and can help you respond to potential challenges from taxing authorities. An ongoing system will help your family avoid the necessity of trying to reconstruct documents and transactions from memory. This might also be helpful in order to avoid unnecessary family disputes.

The paper trail you leave behind will dictate whether family members will have ready access to the information they need in order to finalize your affairs. We recommend having a systematic, organized system that you review and update on a regular basis.

A MATTER OF *Trust*

Chapter 7

Updating, Education and Maintenance

Estate planning is viewed by some as a single transaction, something you do once and then don't have to worry about any more. In addition, the initial planning process may have been emotionally traumatic for the individual or the family and it isn't an experience they want to have to repeat. You may be surprised to learn then, that all estate planning requires ongoing updating, maintenance and family education. Creating the plan is simply the first step in a lifetime process.

There are a number of factors that can influence an estate plan over time:

- Changes in your life, your family or financial circumstances;
- Changes in the law, both state and federal, that may affect the long-term operation of your plan;
- Changes in your lawyer's experience; and
- Changes in the type of legacy you want to leave for the people or organizations you care about.

Changes in Your Life, Family or Financial Circumstances

The first type of change an estate plan faces is change that directly affects you and your family, both personal and financial. There is no way for your attorney and other planning professionals to learn about these changes unless you tell them. These changes can pose a major threat to the success of your plan if your advisors are not aware of them.

The National Network of Estate Planning Attorneys informally polled its clients and discovered that, on average, people update their estate plans every 19.6 years! Has anything changed in the last 20 years that may have affected your estate plan? the last 10 years? the last 5 years? How about in the last year? Estate plans that don't work as expected result in loss of benefits for loved ones, can result in litigation and, at worst, may cause family turmoil that undermines the structure of the family.

Our experience has been that most people don't communicate regularly with their professional advisors, thereby putting their estate plan in danger of failing. Sometimes people are discouraged from communicating with their professional advisors because of the actual or perceived cost of communicating changed circumstances. In other words, people tend to communicate with their advisors less when they know there is an invoice attached.

Changes in the Law

The second type of change an estate plan faces is change to either state or federal laws, including the tax laws with its limitations and restrictions, or other laws that can affect the personal planning protections provided in your estate plan. Judge-made case law can change every time a judge makes a new decision. State and federal statutes change on an on-going basis. How are you keeping up with these changes? Are your advisors providing you with the legal updates that are necessary to ensure that your plan stays current with the changes?

It has been our experience that most estate planning professionals also view estate planning as a one-time event rather than a life-long process. Therefore, many actually disengage their clients at the end of the transaction in the form of a termination or disengagement letter, advising the client that the attorney has no on-going obligation to continue to serve the client's needs. This is an attempt by the legal community to limit their liability to their clients and protect themselves from any ongoing obligation to continue to communicate changes in the law.

Seek out legal and other professionals that are committed to providing their clients with an ongoing means of providing communication, either through regular newsletters, workshops, annual client meetings or a formal updating, education and maintenance process.

Changes in Your Advisor's Experience

The third type of change an estate plan faces is change in your attorney or professional advisor's experience. Many professionals are committed to constantly improving their practices, their knowledge and the quality of their planning. Others continue to practice the same way they always have. Does your attorney have years of cumulative experience or is he or she still doing things the same old way? In Chapter 9—Fiduciaries, Attorneys and Other Scary People—look for guidance on evaluating your attorney's commitment to excellence.

Your estate planning professionals should undertake to stay current on changes in the law as well as changes in practice management and client communication.

Changes in Your Legacy

The fourth type of change you may experience with your estate plan is change in your legacy or the way you want to leave assets to your loved ones or others you care about. These changes may occur as a result of the maturation of your children, the birth of grandchildren, changes in your or your children's marital circumstances or changes in the health or financial well-being of those you love. In addition, you may determine over time and through education that there are asset or creditor protection techniques that can be employed in your planning to protect your loved ones. Whatever the reason, the plan you implement today is unlikely to be the same plan you want to implement for the future.

An Estate Planning Solution—A Three Step Process

It's not about documents—it's about results! The key to proper estate planning is clear, comprehensive, customized instructions for your own care and that of your loved ones. These instructions can be included in a will, in a trust and in several other related legal directives. Regardless of the type of planning chosen, most people are best served with an estate planning process that revolves around a three step process. The process is an approach to planning that recognizes that certain systems have to be firmly in place to create estate plans that work!

The Three Steps

Step 1) Work with a Counselling-Oriented Attorney (as opposed to a word processing-oriented attorney). Much of what passes for estate planning in this country today is little more than word processing! We don't believe you should pay a licensed professional to fill out forms or to do only word processing. The value of a professional is in his or her counsel and advice, based on knowledge, wisdom and experience. If you want an estate plan that works, seek good counselling. (Note: we've incorporated the old English spelling for "counselling," which denotes an approach that focuses on the role of attorney as advisor and counsellor at law.) Maggie had a plan that was boiler-plate word-processing at best.

Step 2) Establish and Maintain a Formal Updating, Maintenance and Education Program. An estate plan faces a myriad of changes. First, there is constant change in your personal, family and financial situation. Second, there are inevitable changes in both federal and state laws that impact your estate plan. Third, there is (or should be) ongoing change in your attorney's experience and expertise. And fourth, your legacy or the way you want to provide for your loved ones may change. Your professional advisors should be continually improving their performance and expanding their knowledge through ongoing education and collective experience. Since everything, except human nature, constantly changes, you cannot expect a plan to accomplish what it is intended to accomplish if it is never updated. The cost of failing to update your plan is typically far greater than the cost of keeping your plan current.

If your attorney doesn't offer a formal updating, maintenance and education program, discipline yourself to review your plan on a systematic basis. As you prepare to have your annual tax return prepared, this is a good time to get out your estate planning documents and review them with your professional team. Financial advisors generally offer or require annual or more frequent reviews with their clients. This gives you a good opportunity to review the performance of your financial portfolio and to discuss and measure whether your investment strategy is still consistent with your long-term goals.

Your family assets should be reviewed on a regular basis to make certain that distributions made during life or upon death will not trigger unintended taxes that your loved ones cannot pay. Meet with your attorney on a regular basis, not to exceed two years, to review your personal estate plan. Include key family members in these meetings, especially those individuals selected to serve as personal representatives, executors or trustees so they can begin the education process and understand the legal issues they may face in the future. Families who take the time to develop a long-term relationship with their legal advisors, who learn and understand the legal concepts that affect their family and who have a commitment to make sure their plan stays updated and maintained have fewer problems when a family crisis arises and estate plans need to be implemented.

Step 3) Assure Fully Disclosed and Controlled Settlement Costs after Your Death. The cost of any estate plan has three distinct parts:

1) Today's Cost: This is what you pay today for counselling and design (or for word processing);
2) The Cost Over Time: This is what you pay over time for updating your plan, or the potentially larger cost of failing to update your plan;
3) The After-Death Cost: This is the cost paid by your loved ones for settlement, administration and distribution of your assets. Regardless of the plan you choose (a will, a trust, or beneficiary designations), there are always after-death costs. Wills are administered through probate; trusts have to be settled or administered and claims have to be made on behalf of named beneficiaries. In any case, assets must be transferred to their intended beneficiaries and final income tax or estate tax returns must be prepared.

Unfortunately, most people only focus on today's costs and often select planning options based on that figure. As a result, they can overlook the updating cost of their plan (or the cost of failing to update their plan) and the after-death estate administration costs. Understanding all of the costs associated with your options and asking how they can be controlled will help you select the option best suited for your personal financial circumstances. Be sure you discuss and understand all three parts of the cost of your estate plan with your attorney before you begin to plan.

The Importance of the Team Approach

Estate planning decisions straddle legal, financial and other advisor categories. Sometimes advisors give conflicting advice—not because the advice is necessarily wrong, but because there can be several ways to achieve a planning goal and the advisors all look at the goal from their own planning perspective, a form of planner "tunnel vision." Tunnel vision, however, can cause unintended consequences.

An example might occur when a non-legal advisor recommends that a parent add an adult child's name to the parent's bank account as a strategy to avoid probate. The parent, child and non-legal advisor might not fully understand that the joint account is potentially subject to the child's creditors if the child faces a divorce or lawsuit, or that joint ownership may interfere with qualification for governmental benefits. Under the circumstances and with proper counsel, the parent might select a different planning strategy to avoid probate.

Sometimes it can seem there are too many options to consider. Some advisors call this "analysis paralysis" to describe the confusion and inaction their clients can experience when there seems to be too many choices. Creating an estate plan is not difficult but it does require a commitment on your part as well as the involvement of all your professional advisors: your attorney, your accountant and your financial and insurance advisors. Depending on your plan, it may also require the participation of a planned giving professional for the charitable organization(s) of your choice.

You should discuss with your advisors how you would like them to work together to help you find the best solutions for your situation. Some advisors are very familiar and comfortable working in a collaborative way to assist their clients. Other advisors may not have had many collaborative experiences. If an advisor is not open to this method, it might say something about whether you will be comfortable with him or her as an advisor.

You should keep your advisors informed of the steps you are taking so each can bring their expertise to the process. This will help you eliminate planning tunnel vision and unintended outcomes. If all of the professionals are included in the planning, you are far more likely to have an estate plan that works; in other words, a plan that meets your goals and keeps you in control of the process and the results.

Ethical Considerations

All of your advisors, but particularly attorneys, must address their ethical duties to each of their clients. The rules that govern attorneys require them to zealously represent the interests of their client. If an attorney represents more than one client on the same matter, even spouses, conflicts of interests can present themselves. You need to know how the attorney can handle those situations without compromising his or her duty to zealously represent you.

The conversation regarding an advisor's ethical obligations should address:

- Whose interests the advisor represents
- How the advisor will present options when the options might create disadvantages for one person at the expense of the other
- Who pays the advisor
- What happens if a conflict of interest occurs
- The scope and manner of disclosing information to other advisors

If spouses or unmarried partners are being represented jointly, you should receive a written confirmation of the details of the attorney's ethical obligations and you may be required to sign a consent form if your attorney represents both parties. It is advisable for spouses (particularly in second marriages) and unmarried partners to retain separate counsel, especially when there is a significant disparity between the individual's wealth, health or extended family since these factors generally will create potential conflicts of interest.

Creating an estate plan that works requires commitment. It also requires an acknowledgment that the plan you create today may not be the plan you need (or want) in the future. Life is dynamic. Your estate plan should be, too. This has never been more true than in the current climate of constant change.

Chapter 8

Taxation

This chapter is intended to provide only a brief overview of some tax considerations that may influence what you might or might not want to do with your estate plan. It cannot be a substitute for a proper review of your specific situation by a tax planning professional.

There are three main categories of taxes that can be triggered when dealing with estates and assets transferred at death. The categories are:

- income taxes, which include earned income, investment income and taxes related to capital gains (or losses)
- gift taxes
- estate taxes, called inheritance or estate transfer taxes in some states, which can include generation-skipping taxes

Whether your estate is subject to one or all areas of these taxes depends on many factors such as your income tax bracket; whether you are married or single, including unmarried couples; whether you live in a community or separate property state; your net worth at your death; whether your state taxes transfers of assets at death, in addition to the federal estate taxes that might be due; and such things as how your planning documents are drafted, how assets are titled and how the plan is administered.

Tax planning is very complex and challenging. The rules change frequently and courts can give conflicting interpretations of the rules. Some advisors focus their practices on tax planning and, indeed, some advisors and their clients can let the "tax tail wag the estate planning dog."

If you have a general understanding of these categories of taxes you will be in a better position to understand the recommendations your advisors might offer and to make good decisions about your estate planning. For instance, failure to consider the tax consequences of gifts you might make during your own lifetime and at death, acquisitions or disposal of assets and other factors can cause you or your survivors to pay more taxes than necessary. Smart planning within the rules will permit you to utilize more assets during your own lifetime and increase the value of assets for your loved ones at your death.

Frequent tax law changes mean it is important to regularly update your plan to make sure it stays current with your goals, circumstances and your net worth. A plan that is not kept current is not going to help you take advantage of opportunities and avoid dangers for yourself and your loved ones.

Income Taxes

Assets held for investment can be invested for growth and/or income. Assets sold at a gain or loss will be subject to income tax rules regarding the gain or loss. If a trust is involved, the income tax might be attributable to the trustmaker or to the trust itself. The general rule is that "grantor trusts," where the trustmaker is the trustee, are taxed to the trustmaker at his or her individual tax rates.

If the trustmaker has given up sufficient control over the trust, as in the case of an irrevocable trust, the income is generally taxed to the trust as a separate entity. Income taxed at trust tax rates often results in higher taxes than if taxed at individual tax rates. There are reasons why a person might opt to assume higher tax rates under a trust rather than the lower individual rates. These reasons generally relate to increased protections from other categories of taxes, increased creditor protections or other desired planning goals.

Gift Taxes

Under the current gift tax rules, annual gifts of up to $11,000 per person per year are excluded from your lifetime gift tax limit—currently $1 million. This means you may make as many gifts totalling $11,000 or less each year to as many individuals as you desire without incurring a gift tax obligation or obligation to file a federal gift tax return (Form 709). Married individuals, on the other hand, can give unlimited gifts to each other and may join together, called "gift-splitting," and give up to $22,000 per year to others before triggering gift tax consequences.

Annual gifts are a strategy to transfer assets from someone with assets over the estate tax applicable exclusion amount (currently $1.5 million), or simply for the purpose of making lifetime gifts that can be enjoyed by others while the gift-giver is still alive and well.

If you are concerned about gift taxes, it is important to coordinate your lifetime gifts with your probable distributions (gifts) at your death to avoid unnecessary taxes. If you anticipate having taxable gifts, you should work with your professional advisors to decide how to minimize them if that one of your estate planning goals.

Estate Taxes

The obligation to pay estate taxes depends on the size of your taxable estate. Currently, if your taxable estate at the time of death is less than $1,500,000, your estate will not be liable for any federal estate taxes. This can be a tricky area, however, because people are not always clear about what is included in their taxable estate.

Generally, we say that everything you own, everything you control and everything your name is on gets included for estate tax purposes. This means that all of your jointly held property gets included (at least a portion of it), everything you own individually, all your life insurance policies (not just the cash value but the death benefit value), your retirement plans including IRAs, 401ks, deferred compensation, and so forth is included in your gross taxable estate. Your taxable estate also includes assets held in other countries.

The "estate tax applicable exclusion amount," also known as the "estate tax exemption" amount, is the amount each person can leave free of estate taxes at death. It is scheduled to increase over the next few years until it is eliminated in the year 2010. However, under the current tax scheme, it is scheduled to return to $1 million in 2011.

Without further government action, the estate tax applicable exclusion amount will be as follows:

2005—$1,500,000
2006—$2,000,000
2007—$2,000,000
2008—$2,000,000
2009—$3,500,000
2010—Unlimited—the estate tax is "repealed," but watch for a new capital gains tax
2011—$1,000,000

In 2005, a single person can leave up to $1.5 million to another completely free of federal estate tax and a married individual can leave an unlimited amount to his or her spouse without incurring any federal estate tax liability. Some states have their own estate or inheritance taxes with different exemption amounts.

Estate taxes are essentially a voluntary tax in the sense that you can "volunteer" to pay them by failing to plan adequately. Avoiding the payment of unnecessary taxes requires education and planning. Seek out the advice of a qualified tax or legal professional to assist you in structuring your estate in a way that will minimize the estate tax effects on your estate. However, make sure understand the trade-off involved with the tax planning recommended to you. You might elect to forego some tax savings strategies in return for some more flexibility and control during life.

One of the advantages that married couples enjoy is the unlimited gifts they can pass to each other during life and at death. Even married couples, however, must plan for what happens to their assets at the death of the surviving spouse if they are concerned about paying unnecessary estate taxes. Couples commonly address this concern by using trusts called by a variety of names: A-B trusts, credit shelter trust, coupon trust, or a trust with marital and family sub-trusts. These terms all mean that the trust was drafted in such a way that the assets in the trust are divided into two sub-trusts at the death of the first spouse. The first sub-trust is commonly called the marital or the A trust. The second sub-trust is called the family or B trust.

The basic premise is that the assets are held in the name of the trust or sub-trusts for the benefit of the survivor at the death of the first spouse. When the survivor dies, the amount held in the trust or sub-trust is either distributed to others named by the trustmaker or remains in trust for the benefit of the named beneficiaries.

The amount of assets the sub-trusts hold can be calculated by a variety of formulas and there is normally an ongoing debate in legal communities about which formula is the best for ensuring that the maximum use of the applicable exclusion amount is obtained. This exclusion amount is sometimes referred to as a "coupon" because it is like having a coupon that is good for a specified amount off of your gross estate before federal estate taxes apply.

Married couples each have a coupon for $1.5 million, which gives them a total of $3 million they can transfer at death if they use their coupons effectively. In addition, they are not penalized if they transfer all or part of their coupon amounts to each other during life or at death. Therefore, married couples have a lot of flexibility when deciding how and when to use their coupons.

The standard instructions incorporated in most trusts for married couples is to have their trusts divide the deceased spouse's trust assets into a marital sub-trust and a family sub-trust. The marital sub-trust is for the benefit of the surviving spouse, and that spouse has access to principal and income from that trust according to the instructions set forth by the trustmaker when the original trust was created.

The family sub-trust is for the benefit of the spouse and children of the couple or, perhaps, some other beneficiaries. The trustmaker can state whether the surviving spouse has full, limited or no access to the principal and income of the family trust. The instructions will also specify the conditions under which the children or other beneficiaries of the family trust will have access to the trust's assets and income.

For instance, the trust instructions can include provisions for dividing the assets into sub-trusts that keep the total assets below the level where federal estate taxes will apply. The trusts can help avoid the issues associated with "he who dies last controls" JTROS property by including instructions to provide for the survivor *and* provide for other beneficiaries at the same time or when the surviving spouse dies.

The other beneficiaries that might benefit from the trust assets do not need to be the same for each spouse, although they frequently are. This mechanism can help spouses avoid the problems previously described regarding married couples with children from prior marriages. If you recall, in that situation the children from the deceased spouse's prior marriage were basically disinherited because all of the assets owned by their father were held in JTROS with the second spouse or she was also the beneficiary of assets held by contract. The survivor spouse did not give any of her husband's assets to his children from that prior marriage, as was his desire.

Generation skipping taxes are another level of tax that may be incurred when the trustmaker elects to "skip" a generation with a gift. To skip a generation doesn't mean that your children won't benefit from your assets, only that they won't be responsible for the payment of any associated estate tax. The estate tax skips to future generations and must be paid upon distribution to that subsequent generation. Currently the generation skipping tax is coordinated or unified with the estate tax and is currently at 1.5 million dollars. Planning for generation skipping taxes is a complex area of the law and consultation with your tax professionals is highly recommended.

The tax law changes are an example of why estate plans must be updated. Although legal and financial advisors can create directives and build plans to withstand many of the anticipated changes in the law, your best interests are served if your estate plan undergoes professional scrutiny from time to time. Chapter 7 discusses updating, education and maintenance of your personal instructions and legal directives.

Chapter 9

Fiduciaries, Attorneys and Other Scary People

It should be abundantly clear that preparing and implementing your estate plan is not an endeavor you should do yourself. You should only work with knowledgeable professionals who have an expertise in estate planning and who encourage you to provide detailed personal information and instructions.

Legal specialization is becoming the norm. Family law attorneys specialize in divorce, child custody and other family law matters. Medical malpractice attorneys work in the area of seeking redress for injuries caused by medical personnel. If you are buying a home, you utilize the services of a real estate attorney. Effective estate planning requires a high degree of specialized knowledge and expertise. Generalists, or "threshold attorneys" (those who take any case that can cross the threshold), won't have the knowledge or expertise necessary to provide comprehensive planning services or the ability to keep pace with future law changes associated with estate planning.

If you have minor children, identifying and selecting a future guardian, conservator or trustee for your child is required. The choice of guardian, conservator or trustee is critical to the future care and well-being of your child, especially after both parents are gone. In addition to selecting who will raise your child consistent with your values and beliefs, families need to give careful thought as to who will manage the money on the child's behalf. The laws pertaining to guardianship, conservatorship and trustees generally vary from state to state. It is important that your choice of trustee—the individual (or individuals) who will be responsible for managing the assets and making distributions be very knowledgeable, skilled and extremely diligent.

Trustees

It is one thing to place resources in a trust, and quite another to manage them in such a way as to last for the period stated in your trust for your beneficiaries. Every trust must have a trustee, someone who will manage the trust's assets.

These are some of the issues you should consider:

- Who will manage the trust assets? The manager of a trust is called a "trustee." A trustee can be any person over eighteen years of age, a bank trust company, a professional trust company, financial planner, a CPA or other professional fiduciary. The trustee holds, administers and distributes all property allocated to the trust for the benefit of the trust beneficiaries according to the trust instructions.

- What skills or qualifications should this person or entity have? Who you select as trustee should be someone who has an aptitude for investments, is detail-oriented and will take the responsibilities of managing your money for the benefit of your beneficiaries very seriously. He or she also needs to be someone who has high attention to detail and enjoys keeping books and records.

Unfortunately, few banks and other trust companies are willing to manage cash assets under several hundred thousand dollars or become as involved in your beneficiary's life as you would wish. In some cases, the cost of administering the trust can outweigh the benefits. Your choices for trustees are varied—you can select an individual, or several individuals to act as trustees, or you can select a bank trust department or a trust organization. In addition, you could select an individual along with a bank trust department or corporate trustee as a co-trustee.

A corporate trustee may also be named as the ultimate successor trustee, the trustee of last resort, even when individuals or family members are initial successor trustees. You never know when an individual or family member will be unable or unwilling to serve in the role of successor trustee and, therefore, it is always good to have a successor trustee category such as a corporate trustee to ensure that a named trustee will always be available to serve. Corporate trustees will be explored in detail in Chapters 10 and 11.

Trusts and trustees are not only used for minor children but also serve a very important function in revocable living trust planning as in Maggie's case. A trustee may serve as a disability trustee, a death trustee during administration or as a trustee for a lifetime trust for your benefit or for the benefit of others you identify as beneficiaries.

Sensitizing Fiduciaries

Guardians, agents, personal representatives and trustees are all "fiduciaries." Fiduciaries can be appointed in a will or in a trust to assume the responsibilities of decision-making in the absence of the primary decision-maker. The manner in which these duties are exercised is of paramount concern to the person making the appointment.

Maggie's experience shows that it is not enough to simply leave the duty or responsibility to a person in whom you have faith or trust. Specific instructions within the estate planning documents can establish a foundation for decision-making and illustrate what you would have done under similar circumstances. The fiduciary can look to those instructions, past actions and decisions for guidance as to the trustmaker's wishes. By doing so you help resolve issues that may otherwise create uncertainty in the mind of the appointed fiduciary. At the same time the laws that govern fiduciaries hold them to one of the highest standards of care. The fiduciary's efforts to meet its legal standards may place it at odds with instructions under a power of attorney, trust or will.

Estate Planning Attorneys

In addition to selecting guardians for minors, personal representatives, executors and pre-need guardians for yourself, it is also important to choose the right estate planning attorney.

Selecting the right estate planning attorney for you means doing your homework—educating yourself, defining your needs, learning to value professional services and seeking guidance in the selection of a qualified individual. The success of your estate planning revolves around your relationship with your estate planning attorney.

Unfortunately, there are many businesses and salespeople masquerading as estate planning professionals. They are inundating the public with sales schemes that involve selling wills, living trusts and other estate planning directives without the involvement of attorneys in the counselling, design and drafting of the plan and, ultimately, the preparation of the directives. Their approach is based on a "transaction" mentality—once you've signed your estate plan, you are done. There is no discussion of the need for ongoing counselling, updating, support and maintenance. Likewise, there is no information being provided regarding the costs of updating, maintenance and then, ultimately, administration of the estate of the person for whom the plan was created.

Proper estate planning requires professional thoroughness by attorneys and other advisors, and respect for the overall well-being of the client and the client's family. Your attorney should aspire to the highest ethical professional behavior that will lend dignity to you, your family and the planning process.

Selecting an Attorney

As you evaluate your needs and begin the search for a qualified attorney, consider the following:

What is an attorney? Attorneys are known by many different names, such as lawyer, counselor or counsellor, solicitor and advocate. Attorneys are required to obtain extensive educational training in order to be prepared and able to represent a client. To qualify to practice law, attorneys must earn a law degree—referred to as a Juris Doctor or J.D.—pass a state bar examination and commit to pursuing continuing legal education for the duration of their legal career. They can also obtain advanced degrees in special categories of law.

Attorneys are subject to codes of ethical conduct and professional responsibility imposed by their state bar associations. Generally, the profession as a whole self-monitors its members.

Attorneys can be sole practitioners, members of small firms or members of large firms. An attorney can be an associate, of counsel or a partner. Attorneys can be general practitioners or attorneys can specialize in a particular area of the law. You should seek an attorney who concentrates his or her practice in estate planning with specific expertise in trust planning.

Attorneys can be plaintiff oriented or defense oriented. They can be trial attorneys, called litigators, with a practice that focuses on trial work, or they can be transactional lawyers who concentrate on some of the non-litigation aspects of the law, such as corporate, real estate or estate planning. Then, there are attorneys who refer to themselves as "relationship oriented" attorneys because they are not merely interested in a client for a single transactional event, but desire an ongoing mutually rewarding and beneficial relationship with their clients.

Selecting an attorney will depend on many different factors—not the least of which is the purpose for which you are interviewing attorneys in the first place. It is important to think about attorneys in the same context as doctors. You wouldn't hire your family practitioner or a gynecologist to conduct brain surgery despite the fact they have the same underlying educational foundation. Additional training and years of specialized experience are determining factors in selecting the right professional for your legal needs.

Selecting the right attorney is critical. However, just seeking a technically competent attorney is often not enough. Consider the personal qualities your attorney should have before you start interviewing

candidates. Things you should look for:
- Scrupulous honesty and integrity
- Sensitive and perceptive communication skills
- Good judgment and common sense
- Discipline and toughness
- Creativity in finding constructive solutions
- Bar affiliations, professional designations, advanced training, and specialization

What does "board certified" mean? Board certification is a voluntary designation program for attorneys. Certification requirements vary depending on your state and the area in which the attorney is seeking certification. Certification often requires additional continuing legal education requirements and may require the applicant to pass a certification examination. There may be additional requirements: that the attorney practice in the area of specialty for a number of years; devote a required percentage of his or her practice to the specialty area; handle a variety of matters in the area to demonstrate experience and involvement; attend ongoing continuing education; and obtain favorable evaluations by fellow lawyers and judges.

Board certification gives you some indication of the attorney's competence in the area for which you are seeking legal advice. This is not to imply that attorneys who are not board certified do not have high levels of competence. Many highly qualified attorneys have chosen for personal or professional reasons not to seek board certification. It does not in any way diminish their qualifications or commitment to excellence in their selected practice area.

Why do I even need an attorney? Can't I do an estate plan on my own? You can try. Many have. Everyone already has an estate plan, whether they know it or not. As we have mentioned several times in preceding chapters, if you fail to plan or if your plan has defects or gaps, the laws in your state of residence will identify the individuals qualified to make decisions for you in the event of your disability or the disposition of your assets in the event of your death.

For some individuals, joint ownership of assets and naming a beneficiary on their life insurance or retirement plan is the only step they've taken toward creating an estate plan. An estate planning attorney can help you avoid some of the pitfalls of the estate planning decisions you might have made or might make. It pays to select your estate planning professional with care, since you will not survive to see whether your plan succeeds, and your loved ones will live with the results.

Your legal professional has spent thousands of dollars and years of time learning how to analyze problems and distinguish the simple from the complex. Finding a simple solution to a complex problem has as much value as unraveling a complex situation that may appear simple. Professionals add value to their services by their knowledge, skill and wisdom, continuing education, independent perspective and willingness to take responsibility for the results.

How do I find an attorney that will be the best for me? This is a serious but not necessarily difficult task. First, consider recommendations from friends and other attorneys. Personal referrals are generally the best way to find out about any type of service you might need, and legal representation is no exception. Talk to other people who are similarly situated. If you belong to any local organizations, consult with other members to obtain a referral. Ask your banker, your CPA, your financial advisor or your current legal services provider. Attorneys rely on good client relations and word-of-mouth references for referral business. If you don't have any success getting a personal referral, consider local or state bar associations, local estate planning councils or other legal referral services.

The Martindale-Hubbell Law Directory is a recognized source of information about attorneys. There are many other directories that list attorneys as well. However, remember that generally the attorneys listed in the directory have paid a fee for the privilege of being listed there and may be merely disguised as advertising vehicles.

As a last resort, let your fingers do the walking and search your local yellow pages. However, understand that you should not select your attorney based solely on yellow page advertising in the attorney section—if such advertising is permitted in your state. You still need to thoroughly consider to whom you should entrust your estate planning.

What kind of questions should I ask? You should ask questions pertinent to your particular area of concern, and you should focus on the following:
- What is your experience in this field?
- Have you handled matters like mine?
- What are the possible problems or concerns in situations like mine?
- How long do you expect this matter to take?
- How will you communicate with me?
- Will you be my only contact, or will anyone else be working with you?
- Is there a charge for the initial consultation? How much?
- Do you offer educational workshops on the subject?
- How do you handle your legal fees? Do you charge by the project? Do you charge a percentage? Do you charge by the hour? What is your hourly rate?
- Beyond fees, what types of expenses should I expect to incur?
- If I need to make changes, how will the fees be handled?
- When will I pay? How often will I receive a bill? If fees are not paid on time, will interest accrue?
- What alternative recommendations can you make?
- Will I sign a formal fee or engagement agreement?
- In the event of a dispute, do you recommend mediation, arbitration or litigation?

How do I make sure my attorney and I have a good relationship? Good legal assistance and advice is not a one-way street. You have to cooperate with your lawyer if you genuinely want him or her to help you. The attorney-client relationship is privileged and confidential, so you need to take a lawyer into your confidence. Here are some important tips:

1) Don't withhold information from your attorney. In the field of estate planning, it is critical your attorney knows everything about you and your loved ones including all of your hopes, dreams, fears, aspirations, eccentricities and peccadilloes. Your attorney needs to know what it is like to be you or a member of your family. What does life look like for your loved ones if you are disabled or if you pass away? What assets do you own, how do you own them and who are the named beneficiaries? What type of planning have you done in the past? Without all of this information, your attorney will be unable to assess your situation, educate you about the law and how it affects you and your family and achieve a result that will be in your best interests.

2) Don't expect simple or immediate answers to complicated questions. Attorneys are justifiably cautious in drawing conclusions or answering complex legal questions without consideration of all the relevant facts. An attorney knows there can be a number of answers to the same question and the law is rarely an "open and shut" case. Attorneys have also been trained to closely examine both sides of an argument. You may find that attorneys frequently use lawyer words like, "it depends," "possibly," "could be" and "there is a great likelihood." Rarely will attorneys use statements such as "guaranteed," "always" and "never." There are frequently a large number of factors that can cause any situation to have an unintended or unexpected outcome.

3) Keep your attorney advised of all new developments. In order to do a good job, your attorney needs to be apprised of facts that may have changed in your personal or financial situation. When your attorney has all the facts, he or she can use this information to provide you with relevant information regarding changes in the law or the attorney's experience.

4) Never hesitate to ask your lawyer about anything you believe is relevant to your situation. Your attorney cannot read your mind. Also, remember that attorneys are not psychiatrists, doctors, marriage counselors or financial advisors. You will still

need a team of trusted advisors to provide you with answers to all of your relevant questions and concerns.

5) Follow your attorney's advice. You asked for it. You paid good money for it. Don't work against your attorney.

6) Be patient. Don't expect instant results. Trust your attorney to follow through and follow up, but don't hesitate to ask for periodic progress reports. You have a right to know exactly what your attorney is doing for you. If you've engaged the services of an estate planning attorney who practices utilizing a formal estate planning process, you should always know what to expect next.

7) Your attorney's primary duty is loyalty to you. His or her interest is protecting your rights and providing you with the highest possible quality of service. Early consultation with an attorney can save you trouble, time and money because:

* The solution to your legal situation may be easily resolved or prevented depending on the nature of your problem.

* The earlier you seek competent advice, the less time is generally needed to complete the work required.

Information is generally more readily available when prompt action is taken. Within the estate planning realm, this may be especially important in the event a person becomes mentally disabled, becomes catastrophically ill or dies before they have completed their planning. Many legal matters or strategies are time sensitive or may have a statute of limitations. Failure to act in a timely manner may prevent you from acting at all.

What if I can't afford a lawyer? Don't assume you can't afford a lawyer. Investigate the matter with competent legal counsel first. In many instances, the cost of competent legal advice now can save you hundreds, if not thousands, of dollars later. If you still feel you can't afford legal help, you may want to consult your local legal aid society.

Attorney Fees and Costs

It is important to understand the fees and billing arrangement before you get a bill. Attorneys' fees can vary dramatically depending on the nature and scope of the legal services provided. You should have a clear understanding of the scope of the representation as to what the attorney will do (or not do), how long it will take, what the attorney will not do without further authorization, what your goals are, and so forth. Financial arrangements should be as clear as possible unless doing so would take longer than what the attorney is retained to do. Even then, the maxim is to "put it in writing."

Some attorneys provide services on a flat-fee, quoted-fee or contingency basis, while others provide services based on an hourly calculation that becomes a function of the attorney's (and his or her staff's) hourly billing rate multiplied by the number of hours expended on your behalf. If you have legal needs of an ongoing nature, will the attorney agree to a retainer fee agreement where you pay a fixed sum each month for services? Are costs included in the quoted fee or will they be in addition to any quoted amounts? Are there any other add-ons like legal research fees, paralegal costs, long distance phone charges or facsimile and copy charges?

Higher hourly fees generally coincide with a lawyer's experience and/or geographic location. For example, an attorney in Los Angeles, Chicago, New York City or Washington, D.C., is likely to charge a higher hourly rate than a comparable attorney in a smaller city. Likewise, the size of the firm may dictate higher hourly rates for both partners and associates than a smaller firm in the same location. Other factors that play into higher fees are the cost of rent, salaries for support staff and firm "perks," or benefits.

Generally, fees are negotiable although, as a rule, not after the services have been provided. If you intend to negotiate with your attorney for the value of the services provided, it would be best to initiate that conversation prior to the onset of the representation. Some attorneys may be offended by the notion they would consider negotiating their fees.

As with any other situation where you will be contracting for professional services, it is recommended you obtain, review and execute a fee agreement or engagement letter that clearly outlines the scope of the representation provided and the billing arrangement to which you've agreed. Some state rules governing attorneys require them to make sure you understand your rights with regard to termination of the relationship and what will happen in the event of a dispute between you and your attorney.

Further, make sure you understand how long the attorney intends to maintain your file. Does the attorney have any processes or procedures for keeping you updated in the event the law changes with regard to the services that have previously been provided?

Other Considerations

Experience. The length of time an attorney has been in practice is an important indicator of his or her success and ability to adequately handle your legal matter. Most attorneys require between three and five years of experience before they have gained reasonable competence in a particular area of the law. Does the attorney regularly attend continuing education on the subject matter? Does he or she teach locally, regionally or nationally? Is he or she published? A good indicator of a person's mastery of a subject is their ability to teach it or to write about it.

Background. Does the attorney have any specific background or experiences that provide him or her with a unique perspective on your situation? Many attorneys are "second career" individuals who may have worked in other professional areas prior to attending law school. This past professional experience may be used to add significant expertise to their area of practice.

Comfort. How does the attorney make you feel? Do you feel comfortable and understood? Does the attorney speak in terms and use language you can understand? Does he or she take the time to explain answers that are still unclear to you?

Work Load. What is the attorney's work load? A common misperception is that an attorney with a cluttered desk is unorganized and has too much work to do an adequate job. Ask the attorney how many clients he or she is currently handling. Does the attorney feel overwhelmed by the work load or outside commitments? What other projects is he or she working on? What are his or her outside interests? Do you feel rushed? Is the attorney taking the time to fully answer all questions regarding your situation? Has the attorney explained the retainer or fee agreement? Do you feel pressured to sign the retainer?

Past Results. Past results are never a guarantee of future success, but knowing an attorney's track record or experience in your type of situation can provide added comfort if he or she has had continuing success in cases similar in nature to yours.

Malpractice Insurance. Some states and some state bar ethics rules require that attorneys include information in their retainer agreements as to whether they carry malpractice insurance. Malpractice insurance is designed to protect you from losses associated with attorney negligence or intentional bad behavior.

Imagination. Does your attorney have the ability to imagine ways in which something might go wrong? If something can go wrong it will and Murphy's Law generally ensures that the one thing that was not planned for is the one thing that will happen.

Skill. Skill includes familiarity with the law, within a technical field or with legal procedures. Skill cannot be taken for granted. Although different attorneys have different skills and skill levels, *any* attorney is legally permitted to handle any legal matter, so long as: 1) there is no conflict of interest; 2) the attorney can handle the matter competently (generally a matter of opinion—the attorney's); and 3) all other laws and rules of professional conduct are followed.

Like other skilled professionals, attorneys develop skills in specific areas of practice. An attorney who is very skilled at matters of type X may need to climb a steep learning curve to properly handle a matter of type Y. Beware of general practitioners or those who have a threshold practice because these individuals, although they may be very good at some legal matters, may not have the specific expertise you need or require. We have discovered that many attorneys, regardless of their practice area, feel competent to draft a simple will. Our experience has been and continues to be that there is no such thing as a simple estate plan, only clients and professionals who don't fully understand the enormity of the problem.

Intuition or "Good Instincts." Intuition may arise from previous encounters with a judge, an opposing attorney or some other decision-maker in the matter at hand. Intuition can give an attorney a sense of how a decision maker is likely to react to various arguments being considered by the attorney. There may be no way to determine whether someone has good intuition, except to rely on your own intuition.

Other factors that will also be important include the resources available to the attorney, the time frame in which the attorney can attend to your matter, and so on. However, ultimately you must be comfortable with your attorney, because your attorney cannot help you unless you communicate with each other. Choose someone you respect, not someone who intimidates you or uses jargon when it isn't needed. Your calls should be answered promptly and professionally. You should not feel as if conversations with your attorney are being either rushed or dragged out. If you are not comfortable, let your attorney know. If the relationship doesn't improve, look elsewhere.

National Estate Planning Organizations

The National Network of Estate Planning Attorneys and WealthCounsel, LLC are alliances of nationally recognized estate planning attorneys from across the country. Together, they provide their membership with the support, education and the tools they need to serve their clients better while building highly successful and rewarding practices.

These organizations support estate planning lawyers on a variety of levels, including:

- Educational and teaching opportunities
- Support from scholars and practitioners
- Practice development and management strategies

Don't discount the value in seeking out organizations and professionals who dedicate themselves to the specialty practice area for which you need advice.

Selecting your personal representative, trustees, attorneys and/or other team members is a critical part of the success of your estate plan. Be sure that you give attention to each detail of your plan and then implement your plan to accomplish your goals.

Other Professional Team Members

In addition to selecting your attorney and your fiduciaries, it is also important to have other competent members on your professional team. These people may include a Certified Public Accountant, financial professional or Certified Financial Planner (CFP) and insurance professional. You can apply the guidelines for selecting and hiring attorneys discussed in this chapter to assist you in your selection of these other important team members.

A MATTER OF *Trust*

Chapter 10

Corporate Trustees

M aggie's story illustrates many of the potential disadvantages associated with using a corporate trustee but it should not serve as an indictment of all corporate trustees. Rather, it should serve as a lesson about the forces that influence the actions of corporate trustees and decisions that must be made when selecting a trustee. It can help a trustmaker understand the checks and balances a trust-based plan should employ to achieve the trustmaker's goals regarding the intended beneficiaries.

Trustees must carry out a long list of responsibilities. Some of these responsibilities are imposed by the terms of the trust itself, as in the case of a trust created for a disabled beneficiary who receives needs-based public assistance benefits. Some responsibilities are associated with the specific nature of the assets in the trust, as in the case of retirement accounts or business interests. Some responsibilities are associated with the trustee's status as a fiduciary which requires strict adherence to standards of care, tax laws and many other rules, regulations and procedures designed to protect beneficiaries and trust assets.

It seems ironic that Maggie did the right thing by creating an estate plan and that she had adequate financial resources to support herself, yet she still fell through the corporate trustee's administrative cracks. Indeed, it can seem that the rules governing trustees are inherently at odds with the needs of beneficiaries. This irony underscores why it is important to understand how the needs of a beneficiary, like Maggie, can be met in the context of the many standards, rules and regulations that come to bear on trustee actions—standards that allow the trustee to meet the literal standards of the trust while remaining blind to the essential purpose of the trust. It also underscores why we must be diligent in incorporating ways to balance the literal meaning of the trust terms against the spirit of the trust and the trustmaker's objectives.

Peruse promotional material for most banks, trust companies and other entities that serve as corporate trustees and you will see a list of the same qualities as their "selling features." There is no doubt that Maggie got the benefit of these features from her corporate trustee. Yet, in retrospect, it is easy to see how some of these features were applied—to a fault.

Experience. Most corporate trustees trumpet their skill at investment management and trust administration as one of their most important attributes. Most corporate trustees have a long history of managing assets for others. Some of the most prominent corporate trustees have been in existence for more than 100 years. They have direct experience and protocols for investing in a variety of assets, including business enterprises and unique assets. They have extensive experience making distributions from trust accounts, preparing tax returns for the trust and beneficiaries, and making sophisticated decisions regarding other requirements of managing trust assets. Their professional management can help build wealth in the trust.

Corporate trustees have departments devoted to specific activities. They have people within their departments whose primary function is to obtain high returns on the invested trust assets and they generally have a large selection of proprietary and other investment choices. They also have high standards regarding the selection of members of the trust department and, therefore, the advice they can offer is considered broad and sophisticated. Their fees are usually tied to the performance of the account based on a percentage of assets under management. Therefore, they have strong financial incentives to maintain good performance and a high investment yield.

As a group, trust department investment advisors have greater experience and resources available to them than most individual trustees are likely to have. The depth of knowledge and experience that a corporate trustee can call upon to manage trust assets is particularly useful regarding trust strategies designed to reduce estate taxes or achieve other tax-sensitive objectives. An individual trustee is not personally likely to have direct experience with a broad variety of asset investments and distribution rules and/or may lack adequate sophistication to make good informed decisions regarding how and when to obtain outside advice.

A corporate trustee is more likely to have dealt with a variety of investment objectives, styles and risk tolerances and can accommodate those differences. An individual trustee might not be able to reconcile his or her personal risk tolerance and investment style with those of the beneficiaries. If the individual trustee is a family member, the potential for intra-family conflict is increased if the clash of style between trustee and beneficiaries cannot be reconciled.

Corporate trustees also have considerable experience in the administration and settlement of estates. They are familiar with probate administration requirements and what must be done to properly administer the trust. Individual trustees rarely have this type of experience and few trusts describe the procedures or mechanisms required to advise the trustee regarding the steps to take to settle the estate.

Well-established management, rules and checks and balances. Trustees must collect and safeguard assets, invest them and administer them to achieve the trustmaker's objectives. The means by which they perform their tasks arise from practical experience garnered through dealings with prior customers and through the need to meet state and federal regulations regarding financial institutions, fiduciaries and trust laws. They must keep accurate records, file tax returns and make distributions from the trust when required. They must also perform many other functions that are ancillary to their investment activities, management and distribution duties.

There are many layers of regulations that corporate trustees must adhere to meet the high standards of management of trust accounts. Corporate trustees must comply with federal and state laws regarding the safety of trust principal, trust income and distributions as well as banking, taxation and other rules. For instance, the Employee Retirement Income Security Act of 1974 (ERISA) and the Taft-Hartley Act of 1947 were designed to govern the management and distribution of retirement accounts held in custodial trust accounts and the Uniform Income and Principal Act, adopted in many states, sets forth parameters within which trustees must operate to protect principal and income on trust accounts.

Federal and state reporting requirements, and the audits that can be triggered as a result, increase the likelihood that trust assets under management by a corporate trustee will be scrutinized and stay within the standards of the law and that mismanagement will be detected early. These laws provide, among other things, that trust assets are to be maintained separate from other bank or trust company assets and, consequently, cannot be used to pay the bank or trust company's creditors or to make loans. Overall, the rules and regulations that govern corporate trustees hold corporate trustees to a higher standard than those to which individual trustees are held or are likely to be able to maintain.

A trustee—corporate or individual—is a fiduciary. As a fiduciary, a trustee cannot "self-deal" or engage in actions that would benefit the fiduciary at the expense of the beneficiaries of a trust. For example, a child might not fully appreciate the conflict of interest presented when acting as trustee under an incompetent parent's trust. The child-trustee might inadvertently compromise their fiduciary standards when faced with the decision about whether to invest assets for income or growth. The fiduciary duty would require distributing income to the beneficiary-parent. Instinct and some self-interest can cause the child to compromise the fiduciary standard and invest for growth which will benefit the child who will ultimately stand to benefit when the parent dies.

Corporate trustees have experience in meeting the high fiduciary standards of prudence and propriety in managing assets for others. Arguably, a corporate trustee employs more checks and balances to guard against violation of the fiduciary standards than might be possible with an individual trustee.

Corporate trustees have extensive operating rules to ensure the likelihood that the trust assets are insulated from losses associated with excessive market, interest and theft risk. They are liable for debts incurred by the trustee through mismanagement of the trust or failure to follow the requirements and standards set by such laws as ERISA. Corporate trustees have financial heft to cover such losses or to carry insurance for such losses. For instance, under ERISA, a corporate trustee would be required to reimburse the trust account for losses due to fraud, theft or errors in managing the trust account. Most corporate trustees have funds earmarked for potential suits associated with or arising out of their trust management.

An individual trustee is not normally required to obtain a bond to insure the execution of his or her trustee duties. As a result, the individual trustee's personal assets can be subject to attachment if they breach their fiduciary responsibility to the beneficiaries. Even where bonding may be required, the individual trustee may still expose personal assets to liability if the losses incurred by the trustee exceed the bond coverage. Consequently, individual trustees might be reluctant to assume such liability and, indeed, some insurance companies can refuse to insure an individual who serves as trustee for a trust. Additionally, an individual's assets or bond might not be sufficient to return the trust account to its pre-loss status.

The many federal and state banking, investment and other regulatory standards that corporations must meet cause corporate trustees to be held to a higher standard than individuals. Therefore, corporate trustees are more likely to be found liable to beneficiaries of a trust if they fail to comply with these laws and regulations.

Of course, adhering to increased regulation can trigger higher costs to maintain compliance standards. The trustmaker should consider the benefits of professional management and regulation against the increased costs of compliance with such regulations. The trustmaker should also keep in mind that individual trustees are not automatically more economical than corporate trustees. The economies a trustmaker hopes to achieve with an individual trustee are reduced if the trustee faces special problems associated with management of a trust and must obtain the services of an attorney and/or accountant. In addition, individual trustees frequently do not make investment decisions that result in a rate of return to the trust that might be obtained by a more experienced corporate trustee.

Continuity. A corporate trustee has past experience, longevity and resources to support a smoother succession or change of trustees when the original individual trustee(s) can no longer serve due to either disability or death or when the trust situs is moved to another region or state. This means that the day-to-day management of assets and trust matters is less likely to be compromised than when a trustee is an individual or family member faced with the emotional fallout of their own decline or at death.

A corporate trustee can efficiently settle a trust when the trust-maker dies because it has performed this function many times before and has the structure to efficiently perform the tasks involved in the final administration of the trust. Settlement of the estate requires not only the typical tasks of inventorying and appraising the assets, but also the preparation of estate tax returns; re-titling trust assets to beneficiaries or successor trusts, according to the trust instructions; and potential liquidation of trust assets to cover estate expenses. An individual trustee is not likely to have been faced with these tasks before and the time associated with settling the estate and administering the trust can be more than the individual is able to handle on his or her own.

Although most properly drafted trusts have a provision for replacing the originally named trustee, most only provide for one or two specifically named successors; thereafter, there should be a mechanism for describing a class of successor trustees that may not be specific individuals known to the trustmaker.

A corporate trustee has an entire department to attend to the needs of the trust account and beneficiaries. If the trust officer who deals with a beneficiary's account falls ill or dies or is unable to serve in the capacity of trustee, another member of the trust department can step into that role without interruption. The transition to a new trustee might not be as smooth in the case of a trust with an individual trustee.

We recently worked with a corporate trustee where the individual assigned to our client had to be out on maternity leave. While absent from her job, another member of the trust department was able to assume her responsibilities and there was no gap in the performance of the trust or with regard to meeting the needs of the beneficiary in her absence. When the trust officer on maternity leave returned to her position full-time, the transition back was equally as smooth. The beneficiary's needs were met at all times without inconvenience or a disruption in service.

Corporate trustees' professional associations can be useful when a beneficiary relocates to a new region or some aspect of the trust account requires attention in another region. For instance, if a beneficiary moves to another region, it can be easier for the beneficiary to maintain the account through a local office of the corporate trustee in the beneficiary's new community than might be possible if the trust had an individual trustee in the old community. A beneficiary who wishes to move to another location might create a hardship for the individual trustee who may have difficulty executing the trustee duties at a long distance.

A trustee must not only be qualified to perform the duties associated with the trust, the trustee must also have the time to do so. Corporate trustees normally have layers of departments with specific responsibilities. The layers can add bureaucracy, for sure, but they can also build in some safety nets to make sure the work of the trust is completed in a timely and competent manner. An individual trustee might not fully appreciate the time required to properly discharge his or her duty to the beneficiaries and to comply with all applicable rules and regulations. Presumably, the individual has added the role of trustee to the other roles he or she already has within their own family, work or home setting and community. An individual trustee may have the best of intentions but if they cannot find sufficient time to devote to trustee functions, they might find themselves neglecting the beneficiary's needs.

Corporate objectivity. The very nature of the standards corporate trustees must meet makes them less vulnerable to pressure from beneficiaries and helps to moderate the biases and emotionality that might exist if the trustee were a family member. Corporate objectivity helps reduce the potential for intra-family conflict that can exist if the trustee is a family member with pre-existing biases and emotional ties to the beneficiaries that may be at odds with his or her duties as trustee.

Corporate trustees are objective—perhaps to a fault. The trustee must respond to the specific goals of the *trust*. This duty might cause the corporate trustee to seem unresponsive to the beneficiaries when the desires of the beneficiaries and the goals of the trust conflict. However, this objectivity can achieve the ultimate goals of the trustmaker. An individual trustee who is subject to the undue influence of others might not achieve the trustmaker's goals as formulated in the language and intent of the trust.

When Do Corporate Trustees Make Sense?

Corporate trustees are usually recommended when the trust is irrevocable, such as a charitable or life insurance trust, or when the trustmaker will be making gifts in trust. The reason is that these trusts are normally used as strategies to reduce federal estate taxes and tax savings can't be achieved if the trustmaker is the trustee of their own trust.

A corporate trustee could be the trustee of choice if the individual trustees the trustmaker would otherwise select are elderly or do not have the time, skills or they do not want to serve as a trustee. A corporate trustee always make sense as the default trustee in the event all named individual trustees are either unable or unwilling to serve.

Fundamental trust law provides that legal ownership (title) and beneficial ownership must be held by different parties. There can be circumstances where the legal ownership and beneficial ownership merge which will cause an end to the trust's function and utility. The use of a corporate trustee prevents this from occurring and provides an added level of protection against unintentional termination of the trust.

Summary

Perhaps Maggie's corporate trustee was indifferent to her needs. Or, perhaps it was sincerely fulfilling its duties—but, as it turns out, only to the letter of the law and not its spirit. Few stories such as Maggie's are black and white.

Perhaps, in this environment of perpetual mergers of financial institutions and the move away from locally owned and operated banks, it is unrealistic to expect that any corporate trustee could have a personal connection with the beneficiaries of the trusts they manage. It can be difficult to keep up with the changes in your bank's name much less the people employed by them.

Every selling feature appearing in corporate trustee websites and brochures is a potential detriment. The good news is that the layers of departments in a corporate trustee setting help support good, sound financial management of trust assets, continuity and stability. The bad news is that these same layers can create a bureaucracy that insulates the trustee from the beneficiary's immediate personal needs. The good news is that corporate trustees receive compensation based on their success with investments. The bad news is that the corporate trustees can be reluctant to make changes that would result in a decrease in the assets managed, such as distributions to beneficiaries.

The good news-bad news perspective is equally applicable to individual trustees. The good news is that individual trustees can be in a better position to deal with the beneficiary on a personal basis. The bad news is that "familiarity can breed contempt." The trustee might impose personal biases upon the beneficiary, as in the case of investment styles and risk tolerances. The beneficiary might resent the trustee who fails to respond in particular ways because the trust document does not permit that response. This has the potential to cause significant intra-family conflict in the case of family members who are trustees and such conflict can undermine the functions the trustee was selected to perform.

Some will read Maggie's story and blame the corporate trustee for being unfeeling and insensitive to Maggie's situation and conclude that corporate trustees should be avoided, but that would be missing the point. Corporate trustees perform much needed functions and it is important to understand how they are as much the victims of the rules that govern their activities as is the beneficiary who must rely on their actions.

If Maggie's daughter had been living when Maggie created her trust, she would have named Pat as her successor trustee. Maggie probably never anticipated that she would outlive her daughter. If she had prudently included a default clause in the trust to empower a corporate trustee to oversee her affairs if something should happen to her successor she would have found herself in the same situation she ultimately ended up in—her trust did not have sufficient directions or mechanisms to maintain the personal element in her care and comfort.

Large families may have a ready supply of family members who can fill the role of individual successor trustee to ensure that there is a personal perspective regarding the beneficiary. Smaller families have a smaller pool of successor candidates which means that other mechanisms should be used to maintain the personal perspective. In either case, the trustmaker and their advisors should consider Maggie's story and discuss "what if" scenarios and provide a good statement of the trustmaker's intent to guide trustees for all times.

The selection of individual trustees versus corporate trustees does not need to be an all or nothing proposition. One solution is for the trustmaker to create a panel of trustees to bring the best qualities of both categories of trustees to manage and administer the trust for the beneficiary. In this way, the strong management and rule compliance qualities of the corporate trustee can be combined with the personal relationship and attention of the individual trustee. Maggie's story can provide some insights about where to build in extra protections regarding the division of trustee powers and duties and mechanisms needed to ensure that the personal element is not lost due to inherent corporate bureaucracy.

The trustmaker should take pains to explain his or her intent regarding the use and preservation of trust assets for their own needs

A MATTER OF 𝒯rust

and later beneficiaries. These later beneficiaries are called "remainder" beneficiaries because they will take what remains after the first beneficiary(ies) stops receiving benefits under the trust.

As discussed in prior chapters, a clear and detailed statement of the trustmaker's intent can provide a good compass point against which trustees, corporate and/or individual, can determine which actions are appropriate and are consistent with the trustmaker's objectives. If the matter should ever require court intervention, the court will have the statement of intent to guide it in disposition of the matter. Otherwise, the court will be required to apply established trust principles that might have no correlation with the trustmaker's actual objectives. The court will have little or no discretion to infer a trustmaker's intent where none is stated.

Maggie's story carries another lesson—the need to follow a program of regular updating and maintenance of your estate plan. The need for a formalized plan of updating and maintenance is more fully addressed in Chapter 7—Updating, Education and Maintenance.

A MATTER OF *Trust*

Chapter 11

Interviews with Corporate Trustees

Selecting a corporate trustee might be intimidating for many people. However, you should approach this process in the same way you select any other professional—by getting referrals from people whose judgment you trust, checking references, performing an independent review of the trustees' credentials and through personal interviews with trust personnel.

Most of us have had prior experience getting referrals to physicians, attorneys and financial advisors. The referrals can come from legal and financial planning advisors or family and friends who have experience with specific trust companies. The internet can provide assistance and be useful in obtaining information you need to know about the trustees' credentials, financial resources and services offered.

The personal interview is not something most people perform even before engaging the services of a physician, financial advisor or lawyer. The following are some guidelines for conducting this interview. This list is not exhaustive, however, and there are no right or wrong answers. You should take note of the ease or lack of ease with which you obtain an appointment with your corporate trustee candidates and this should be but one of the factors you should weigh in the decision-making process. If the trustee candidate is reluctant to schedule such an appointment with you or if you must navigate several layers of bureaucracy to get to the decision-maker for an appointment, you should consider whether this is what you and/or your beneficiaries might experience from the trustee when the "honeymoon is over."

Some specific questions you might ask a corporate trustee are listed below. You should consider interviewing numerous corporate trustees to gain experience in the types of corporate trustees available to you and the variety of services they can offer. This can only cost you some time and effort but will serve you well in deciding how to create your directives for the best possible fit in the event you must rely on the services of a corporate trustee.

Some questions to consider:
- How long have you been providing trustee services?
- Describe your typical trust client.
- What is the amount of your average trust account?
- How do you balance the needs of the primary beneficiary against those of the secondary and remainder beneficiaries?
- What are the top distinguishing features of your company?
- What type of services do you provide?
- How are your services or the manner in which you provide them different or better than your competitors?
- Who are your competitors?
- In what ways do they perform services better than your company? In what ways does your company perform services better than your competitors?
- Has your company acquired other organizations or has your organization been acquired by others since its founding? Who, when and what result?
- What is the average length of service for a trust officer with your company?
- How many trusts do you personally manage or oversee, on average?
- What is the average ratio of trust officers to beneficiaries and trust accounts over the last 25 years?
- What is the "chain-of-command" within the trust company?
- What is the process for making trust distribution decisions?

- How long does this decision-making process take?
- What is the appeal process if a beneficiary disagrees with a decision of the trustee?
- How many trust accounts have you lost over the last 10 years?
- How many trust accounts have you gained over the last 10 years?
- What is the average size of the trust accounts you manage?
- What is the smallest account size you will accept? What happens if my trust assets fall below that level?
- How many offices do you have and where are they located?
- How often do you have face-to-face meetings with the beneficiaries of the trust accounts? Will you meet more often by request?
- What mechanism do you have to make personal contact with the beneficiary of a trust?
- What is your fee structure for handling trusts? Is there a set-up or termination fee?
- Are there fees for extraordinary services? How are those services priced and communicated?
- What percentage of trust assets are invested in funds or financial assets that are proprietary?

Summary

You should not limit your questions to this list. You should feel free to ask a trustee candidate anything and everything you need to know to feel comfortable with them as your agent. You should consider how someone, an institutional "someone," would follow your instructions. Find out by asking and learning how corporate trustees work, where you need to fill-in blanks and provide mechanisms for following your instructions. The more questions you ask, the more likely you will receive information from potential trustees that will guide you in drafting directives and letters of instructions that serve the purpose for which they were designed—in the spirit of the law as well as in the letter of the law.

Chapter 12

Conclusion

Maggie's story provides insights into where to build in extra guidance and protections regarding the "care and feeding" of the beneficiary of a trust. It can guide the trust drafter regarding the division of trustee powers and duties and mechanisms needed to ensure that the personal element is not lost in the inherent bureaucracy associated with corporate trustees.

The trust creator and advisors should take pains to explain the creator's intent regarding the use and preservation of trust assets for the creator/beneficiary and later beneficiaries. A clear and detailed statement of the trustmaker's intent can provide a good compass point against which trustees, corporate and/or individual, can determine which actions are appropriate and in keeping with the trustmaker's objectives. If the matter should ever require court intervention, the court will have, at a minimum, a statement of intent by the trust's creator to guide it in disposition of the matter. Otherwise, the court will be required to apply established trust principles which might have no correlation with the trustmaker's objectives. The court will have little or no discretion to infer a trustmaker's intent where none is stated.

In addition to underscoring the importance of personal instructions, Maggie's story also underscores the importance of all of the elements of good, sound estate planning. These elements include good counselling, asset integration and a formal education, updating and maintenance program supported by a team of professional advisors. These elements can be the best insurance for a solid estate plan that is designed to remain a good fit over your lifetime, through good health and bad, and to achieve your goals for yourself and your loved ones.

We wish you the best!

Glossary of Estate Planning Terms

Administrator — Person named by the court to administer a probate estate. Also called an Executor or Personal Representative.

Agent — An individual named in a power of attorney with authority to act on the power giver's behalf. Has a fiduciary responsibility to the power giver.

Ancillary Administration — An additional probate in another state. Typically required when you own assets or real estate in a state other than the state where you live that is not titled in the name of your trust or in the name of a joint owner with rights of survivorship.

Basis — What you paid for an asset. Value used to determine gain or loss for capital gains and income tax purposes.

Buy-Sell Agreement — A written agreement between co-owners of a business to determine the rights of the owners in the event of retirement, disability or death.

Co-Trustees — Two or more individuals who have been named to act together in managing a trust's assets. A Corporate Trustee can also be a Co-Trustee.

Corporate Trustee — An institution, such as a bank or trust company, that specializes in managing or administering trusts.

Disclaim — To refuse to accept a gift or inheritance so it may be transferred to the next recipient in line. Must be done within nine months of the date-of-death.

Durable Power of Attorney for Financial Matters — A legal document that gives another person full or limited legal authority to make financial decisions on your behalf in your absence. Valid through mental incapacity. Ends at revocation, adjudication of incapacity or death.

Durable Power of Attorney for Healthcare — A legal document that gives another person legal authority to make healthcare decisions for you if you are unable to make them for yourself. Also called Healthcare Proxy, Healthcare Surrogate or Medical Power of Attorney.

Estate Administration — The process of settling either a probate estate or trust estate. There are generally three steps that include identifying the assets, paying the debts of the estate and distributing the balance to the beneficiaries.

Executor — Another name for Personal Representative.

Fiduciary — Person having the legal duty to act for another person's benefit. Requires great confidence, trust, and a high degree of good faith. Usually associated with a Trustee or Personal Representative.

Funding — The process of re-titling and transferring your assets to your Living Trust. Also includes the re-designation of beneficiaries to include your Living Trust as a beneficiary. Sometimes called asset integration.

Inter vivos — Latin term that means "between the living." An *inter vivos* trust is created while you are living instead of after you die. A Revocable Living Trust is an *inter vivos* trust.

Irrevocable Life Insurance Trust (ILIT) — An irrevocable trust for the purpose of holding title to life insurance. Used as an advance planning technique to remove the death benefit proceeds of life insurance from an insured's gross taxable estate.

Irrevocable Trust — A trust that cannot be changed or canceled once it is set up. Opposite of a Revocable Living Trust. Can be created during lifetime or after death.

Intestate — Dying without a Will.

Joint Ownership — When two or more persons own the same asset.

Joint Tenants with Right of Survivorship — A form of joint ownership where the deceased owner's share automatically and immediately transfers to the surviving joint tenant(s) or owner(s).

Living Trust — A legal entity created during your life, to which you transfer ownership of your assets. Contains your instructions to control and manage your assets while you are alive and well, plan for you and your loved ones in the event of your mental disability and give what you have, to whom you want, when you want, the way you want at your death. Avoids guardianship of the property and probate only if fully funded at incapacity and/or death. Also called a Revocable *Inter Vivos* Trust.

Limited Liability Company (LLC) — A form of legal entity that can provide limited liability from the claims of creditors. Can be taxed as a sole proprietorship, partnership or corporation.

Living Will — A legal document that sets forth your wishes regarding the termination of life-prolonging procedures if you are mentally incapacitated and your illness or injury is expected to result in your death.

Personal Representative — Another name for an Executor or Administrator.

Pour Over Will — An abbreviated Will used with a Living Trust. It sets forth your instructions regarding guardianship of minor children and the transfer (pour over) of all assets owned in your individual name (probate assets) to your Living Trust.

Power of Attorney — A legal document that gives another person legal authority to act on your behalf for a stated purpose. Ends at revocation, incapacity (unless it is a durable power of attorney) or death.

Probate — The legal process of validating a Will, paying debts, and distributing assets after death. Generally requires the services of an attorney.

Probate Estate — The assets owned in your individual name at death (or beneficiary designations payable to your estate). Does not include assets owned as joint tenants with rights of survivorship, payable-on-death accounts, insurance payable to a named beneficiary or trust, and other assets with beneficiary designations.

Probate Fees — Legal, executor, court, and appraisal fees for an estate that requires probate. Probate fees are paid from assets in the estate before the assets are fully distributed to the heirs.

Revocable Living Trust — Another name for a Living Trust.

Spendthrift Clause — Protects assets in a trust from a beneficiary's creditors.

Successor Trustee — Person or institution named in a trust document that will take over should the first trustee die, resign or otherwise become unable to act.

Testamentary Trust — A trust created in a Will. Can only go into effect at death. Does not avoid probate.

Testate — An estate where the decedent died with a valid Will.

Trust Administration — The legal process required to administer trust assets after incapacity or death. Includes the management of trust assets for the named beneficiaries, the payment of debts, taxes or other expenses and the distribution of assets to beneficiaries according to the trust instructions. Generally requires the services of an attorney.

Trustee — Person or institution who manages and distributes another's assets according to the instructions in the trust document.

Will (or Last Will & Testament) — A written document with instructions for disposing of assets after death. A Will can only be enforced through the probate court.

A MATTER OF *Trust*

Appendix B

Estate Planning Checklist

Part 1—Communicating Your Wishes

☐ Yes ☐ No   Do you have a will or trust?

☐ Yes ☐ No   Are you comfortable with the executor(s) or trustee(s) you have selected?

☐ Yes ☐ No   Have you executed a living will or healthcare proxy in the event of catastrophic illness or disability? Are your important family members named in these documents as your surrogate for decision making purposes?

☐ Yes ☐ No   Have you executed a durable financial power of attorney for the purpose of appointing an agent to handle your financial affairs in the event of your disability?

☐ Yes ☐ No   Have you considered a revocable living trust to consolidate assets, avoid probate, minimize exposure to estate tax and provide long-term protections for your spouse and other loved ones?

☐ Yes ☐ No   If you have a living trust, have you titled your assets in the name of the trust? Have you named your trust as the primary beneficiary on your contract assets such as insurance, annuities, and retirement plans.

☐ Yes ☐ No   If you have a will, trust or other legal directives, have they been reviewed in the last two years to ensure they are consistent with your wishes, the status of the law and your attorney's changing experience?

Part 2 — Protecting Your Family

☐ Yes ☐ No   Does your will name a guardian for your minor children?

☐ Yes ☐ No   Does your estate plan specifically include provisions to protect your spouse and other loved ones in the event of your death?

☐ Yes ☐ No   Are you sure you have the right amount and type of life insurance to help with survivor income, loan repayment, capital needs and estate-settlement expenses?

☐ Yes ☐ No   Have you considered an irrevocable life insurance trust to exclude the insurance proceeds from being taxed as part of your estate?

☐ Yes ☐ No   Have you considered creating trusts for either your spouse, partner or other family to facilitate gift giving?

Part 3 — Helping to Reduce Your Estate and Income Taxes

☐ Yes ☐ No   Do you and your spouse each individually own enough assets for each of you to qualify for the applicable exclusion amount, currently $1.5 million?

☐ Yes ☐ No   Are both your estate plan and your spouse's designed to take advantage of each of your applicable exclusion amounts, currently $1.5 million?

☐ Yes ☐ No   Are you making gifts to family members or others that take advantage of the annual gift tax exclusion, currently $11,000?

☐ Yes ☐ No   Have you gifted assets with a strong probability of future appreciation in order to maximize future estate tax savings?

☐ Yes ☐ No   Have you considered charitable trusts that can provide you with both estate and income tax benefits?

Part 4 — Protecting Your Business

☐ Yes ☐ No   If you own a business, do you have a management succession plan?

☐ Yes ☐ No   Do you have a buy-sell agreement for your family business interests?

☐ Yes ☐ No   Is your spouse employed by your business? Have you taken all steps necessary to ensure his or her continued participation in the business in the event of your death?

☐ Yes ☐ No   Have you considered a gift program that involves your family-owned business?

COORDINATE YOUR DIRECTIVES TO CONTROL YOUR ASSETS

PROBATE	OPERATION OF LAW	CONTRACT
WILL 'NO WILL PROBATE" [intestate succession = states probate laws say who gets what]	JTWROS TBE TOD	INSURANCE POD RETIREMENT ACCOUNTS IRAs TRUSTS
Only controls assets that are 1.) titled in your individual name and 2.) that have **no** built-in survivorship feature.	Has built-in survivorship feature that tells who gets the asset at owners death. **WARNING!** If there is a defect in title, asset must go through probate to decide who gets asset under will or 'no will" probate.	Has built-in survivorship feature that tells who gets the asset at owners death. **WARNING!** If there is a defect in beneficiary designation(s), the asset might have to go through probate to decide who gets the asset under the will or 'no will" probate if the terms of the contract dont have a default recipient provision.
	Go to probate de: in designation.	Go to probate de: in designation.

DISABILITY DIRECTIVES

WHAT ARE YOUR INSTRUCTIONS?

WHO IS AUTHORIZED TO SPEAK & ACT FOR YOU WHEN YOU ARE UNABLE TO COMMUNICATE YOUR WISHES?

HEALTH	FINANCES
♦ Living Will	♦ Durable Financial Power of Attorney
♦ Durable Healthcare Power of Attorney	♦ Alternate or Dual Agent(s)?
♦ HIPAA	♦ General or limited powers?
♦ Durable Mental Healthcare Power of Attorney	♦ Springing or Immediate Effect?
	♦ Unlimited or Limited Gifting Powers?
♦ Organ Donation Form	
♦ Living Trust	♦ Living Trust
♦ Guardian Nomination (for yourself)	
Default plan, if you dont make one: State laws/court.	Default plan, if you dont make one: State laws/court.

Other Considerations:

Where to keep originals?
Only useful if available. Copies & repositories [e.g., Docubank, www.docubank.com].

Paper trail: Location list.

Amendments and revocation.

A MATTER OF *Trust*

Appendix C

Resources

AARP: 1-800-424-3410; *www.aarp.org*. Ask for a copy of *Product Report: Wills & Living Trusts*. AARP does not sell or endorse living trust products.

Aging With Dignity: 888-5WISHES (594-7437); *www.agingwithdignity.org*

Council of Better Business Bureaus, Inc., 4200 Wilson Blvd., Suite 800, Arlington, VA 22203-1838; 703-276-0100; *www.bbb.org*

Ethical Wills: *www.ethicalwill.com*

My Personal Wishes, LLC: P.O. Box 583, Boys Town, NE 68010; *www.mypersonalwishes.com*

SunBridge, Inc.: 8238 Westminster Abbey Blvd., Orlando, Florida 32835; *www.sunbridgestrategies.com*

The American Bar Association, Service Center, 541 N. Fairbanks Ct., Chicago, IL. 60611; 312-988-5522; *www.abanet.org*.

The National Academy of Elder Law Attorneys, Inc., 1604 North Country Club Rd., Tucson, AZ 85716; 520-881-4005; *www.naela.org*

The National Consumer Law Center, Inc., 18 Tremont St., Ste. 400, Boston, MA 02108-2336; 617-523-8010; *www.consumerlaw.org*

The National Network of Estate Planning Attorneys, Omaha, NE; *www.nnepa.com*

Tribute Direct: 15415 International Plaza Drive, Suite 120, Houston, TX 77032-2448; 800-994-3070; *www.tributedirect.com*

WealthCounsel, LLC, P.O. Box 68449, Portland, OR 97268-0449; 888-659-4069; *www.wealthcounsel.com*

Suggested Reading

All My Children Wear Fur Coats—How to Leave a Legacy for Your Pet; **Peggy R. Hoyt;** Legacy Planning Partners, LLC; 254 Plaza Drive, Oviedo, Florida 32765; 407-977-8080; www.LegacyForYourPet.com.

Special People, Special Planning—Creating a Safe Legal Haven for Families with Special Needs; **Peggy R. Hoyt and Candace M. Pollock;** Legacy Planning Partners, LLC; 254 Plaza Drive, Oviedo, Florida 32765; 407-977-8080; www.SpecialPeopleSpecialPlanning.com.

Loving Without a License—An Estate Planning Survival Guide for Unmarried Couples and Same Sex Partners; **Peggy R. Hoyt and Candace M. Pollock;** Legacy Planning Partners, LLC; 254 Plaza Drive, Oviedo, Florida 32765; 407-977-8080; www.LovingWithoutALicense.com.

A Guide to Recalling and Telling Your Life Story; **Hospice Foundation of America;** 800-854-3402

Invest in Charity: A Donor's Guide to Charitable Giving; **Ron Jordan and Katelyn Quynn;** ISBN# 0471717395

Living with the End in Mind: A Practical Checklist for Living Life to the Fullest by Embracing Your Mortality; **Erin Tierney Kramp;** available on Amazon.com.

Appendix D

Personal Legacy and Ethical Wills

Here are some ideas to help you get started writing your personal legacy or ethical will:

Collect ideas—a few words or a sentence or two about things like:

- Your beliefs and opinions
- Things you did to act on your values
- Something you learned from grandparents/parents/siblings/spouse/children
- Something you learned from experiences that you want to share
- Mistakes you have learned from
- Things you are grateful for
- Your hopes and dreams for the future
- Your definition of success
- Why you love certain people and will miss them
- What you appreciate most about people, life, experiences
- What spirituality means to you
- Your happiest moments
- Your funniest moments
- Information about your heritage
- Challenges you've faced and what you learned from the experience

Write about important events in your life:

- Imagine that you only have a limited time left to live. What would you regret not having done? What life experiences do you cherish?
- Save items that articulate your feelings, e.g., quotes, cartoons, etc Consider including:
- Words of praise to those who deserve it
- An apology (if necessary)
- A request for forgiveness (if necessary)
- An offering of forgiveness (if necessary)
- Words of wisdom (without lecturing)
- An honest attempt to settle unresolved issues and disputes

There's no perfect time (like the present) to write your personal legacy declaration but certain events in your life may motivate you to consider getting started such as:

- Starting a new life with someone
- Having a baby
- After a divorce
- At milestones in your children's lives
- When all your children have left home
- At retirement
- At the end of your life

Memorial Letter

and Special Instructions for My Family

To My Loved Ones:

General Purpose of This Letter

This letter is written in order to share my feelings with my personal representative and loved ones about my general memorial wishes and special instructions.

Conflict with My Last Will and Testament

If the feelings I express in this letter are in conflict with any of the provisions of my Last Will & Testament, the provisions of my Last Will & Testament shall control and the provisions of this letter shall be void and of no effect.

Final Instructions

I have included in this letter my desires and wishes. It is my hope that my survivors implement my wishes when making my final arrangements.

My Desires for My Final Arrangements

1) *After my death, I prefer:*

☐ **CREMATION**

_____ In an urn of my choosing:_____

_____ Scatter my ashes

        Where:_____

        By whom:_____

_____ Special Requests:_____

_____

_____ I have no preference

☐ **A TRADITIONAL BURIAL**

_____ In a plot located in (cemetery name):_____

        Address:_____

        Plot location:_____

_____ At a place my family determines

_____ Other:_____

_____ I want to wear:_____

_____ I have no preference.

☐ **MAUSOLEUM**

Name:_____

Address:_____

Contact Name:_____

☐ **NO PREFERENCE**

_____ I have no preference regarding cremation, burial
or mausoleum.

2) I want the following type of funeral service (indicate as many as desired)

☐ Church/religious _____

_____
(name and location of church)

☐ Funeral home service: _____

☐ Memorial service to be held at: _____
_____ With viewing
_____ No viewing
_____ Graveside service
_____ Other: _____

3) I would like the following (indicate as many as desired):

_____ Clergy: _____
_____ Flowers: _____
_____ Donations in lieu of flowers sent to: _____

_____
_____ Pallbearers: _____

_____
_____ Military Honors: _____
_____ Music: _____
_____ Prayers or special requests: _____
_____ Gathering after the service: _____

_____

4) I want my headstone to read:

_____

_____

_____

5) I want my obituary to read:

_____

_____

_____

*6) I would like the following parting words to be read at my
final service:*

_____

_____

_____

_____

_____

(Here are some possibilities for starting this piece: "You know I
always like to have the last word, so here it is..." or "I guess you
know why we're here..." or "I never liked being the center of
attention, but here we are..." or "Don't cry for me...")

7) Other desires or wishes:

_____

_____

_____

_____

_____

Your Signature:_____

Date:_____

About The Authors

PEGGY R. HOYT, J.D., M.B.A.

Peggy is the oldest of four daughters born to John and Trudy Hoyt. She was born in Dearborn, Michigan, and spent her first ten years as a "PK," or "preacher's kid," before her father joined The Humane Society of the United States. Peggy graduated with an A.A. degree from Marymount University in Arlington, Virginia; earned a B.B.A. and M.B.A. from Stetson University in DeLand, Florida; and earned a J.D. from Stetson University College of Law in St. Petersburg, Florida.

Today, Peggy and her law partner, Randy Bryan, own and operate Hoyt & Bryan, LLC. Her law firm limits its practice to estate planning and administration for individuals, married couples and life alliance partners, including special needs planning, pet planning, elder law and guardianships. She also works in the areas of business creation, succession and exit planning, as well as real estate, corporate and equine law.

Peggy is the author of a one-of-a kind book called *All My Children Wear Fur Coats—How to Leave a Legacy for Your Pet,* available through her law office, your favorite bookstore or by visiting www.LegacyForYourPet.com. In addition, she and Candace Pollock are co-authors of *Special People Special, Special Planning—Creating a Safe Legal Haven for Families with Special Needs* and *Loving Without a License—An Estate Planning Survival Guide for Unmarried Couples and Same Sex Partners.* All of these books are available through their law offices, your favorite bookstore or by visiting www.SpecialPeopleSpecialPlanning.com. and www.LovingWithoutALicense.com.

She is active in a variety of organizations, including the National Network of Estate Planning Attorneys WealthCounsel, Apex Expeditions, Sunbridge Strategies and the Central Florida Estate

Planning Council. She is a regular speaker on team training and estate planning topics and is also a contributor of practice management materials. In addition, she serves as trustee to Stetson University's Business School Foundation and serves on the executive council of the General Practice, Solo and Small Firm section as well as the Animal Law Committee of the Florida Bar. Peggy is also an advisory board member to 2ndChance4Pets, a not-for-profit organization dedicated to assisting seniors and their pets (www.2ndchance4pets.org and www.petgardian.com).

Peggy lives with her husband, Joe Allen in Central Florida. Her passion is her pets and she enjoys spending her "free" time playing with her wild mustang horses, Reno and Tahoe, and her Premarin rescue, Sierra; her dogs, Kira, Corkie, Tiger and Fiona; and her cats, Beijing, Bangle, Cuddles, Tommy, Shamu and Spook.

CANDACE M. POLLOCK, J.D.

Prior to attending law school, Candace owned a business that provided claim review and consulting services to Ohio lawyers in the area of workers' compensation and Social Security claims— areas involving the rights of disabled people. During this period she was a founding member and first acting president of the Women Business Owner's Association (now known as the Cleveland Chapter of the National Association of Women Business Owners).

Candace was encouraged to attend law school by her attorney-clients and graduated from Cleveland-Marshall College of Law in 1986. After graduation, she joined Hahn & Swadey—a firm established in 1951—and later became partner in the firm that ultimately became HAHN & POLLOCK, LLC.

Candace continued representing disabled people while expanding her practice to include estate and financial planning, probate and elder law services in response to the needs of her clients.

Her participation in professional and community activities

includes leadership roles in legal and professional associations, including chair of the Workers' Compensation and Social Security Section of the Cuyahoga County Bar Association, representative-at-large on the board of trustees of the Ohio Academy of Trial Lawyers (OATL), and Member of the Executive Committee of the Workers' Compensation Section of OATL. She has participated in a broad range of organizations including board and non-board positions in non-profit, charitable and political organizations.

She is currently a mentor coach in the Practice Builder Program of the National Network of Estate Planning Attorneys (NNEPA). In this national program, she helps coach attorneys in effective business management and marketing practices to help them create practices that meet the needs of their clients and families.

Candace and Peggy Hoyt co-authored *Special People, Special Planning—Creating a Safe Legal Haven for Families with Special Needs* and *Loving Without a License—An Estate Planning Survival Guide for Unmarried Couples and Same Sex Partners.* They are available as speakers and for interviews and are happy to contribute written material to publications regarding planning for special people.

In addition to her professional and community activities, she teaches individuals and organizations about various estate planning and disability planning topics.

Candace resides in Cleveland, Ohio with her life alliance partner, Hutch, and their animal family.

JACQUELINE J. POWERS

Jacqueline makes her home in Orlando, Florida. She is retired and spends her time traveling and helping her neighbors and friends.

In October 1999, during the closing of the former Naval Training Center, Orlando, Florida, Jacqueline trapped approximately 100 cats. She had them spayed or neutered and all received rabies and distemper shots. In addition, she found homes for these cats so none were destroyed by animal services. She now volunteers with C.A.T.S.—C.A.N., INC., "Caring about Today's Strays—Cat Adoption Network." Their online address is www.marrow.org. She also volunteers with A Gift of Hope for Medically Fragile & Cancer Children, Inc. Visit their website at www.kidsbeatingcancer.com.

Contact Us

Peggy and Candace are available as speakers and for interviews and are happy to contribute written material to publications regarding estate planning and trusts:

HOYT & BRYAN, LLC	HAHN & POLLOCK, LLC
254 Plaza Drive	820 West Superior Avenue, Suite 510
Oviedo, Florida 32765	Cleveland, Ohio 44113
(407) 977-8080 (T)	(216) 861-6160 (T)
(407) 977-8078 (F)	(216) 861-5272 (F)
peggy@HoytBryan.com	info@HAHNPOLLOCK.com
www.HoytBryan.com	www.HAHNPOLLOCK.com

Other Planning Concerns

Pets. For information related to planning for your pets, please visit www.LegacyForYourPet.com.

Special Needs. If you have a special needs family member, please visit www.SpecialPeopleSpecialPlanning.com.

Unmarried Couples and Same Sex Partners. Unmarried people have unique planning concerns. Visit www.LovingWithoutALicense.com for more information.